Letters to the Editor:

Opinions, Objections, and Recollections

By Richard Lettis, Ph.D.

To Lucy, *sine quae non*

Introduction 1
Format 3
1975 4
1977 10
1978 14
1979 17
1980 21
1984 27
1986 29
1989 32
1994 33
1996 34
1998 39
2001 41
2003 42
2006 44
2007 52
2008 56
2009 62
2010 80
2011 95
2012 121
2013 142
2014 158
2015 197
2016 230
About the Author 233
Index 234
Acknowledgments 239

Introduction

I hope I'm not biased by age, but I think that when we are younger we are more given to the delights of disparagement, not infrequently unjustified, than we do in later years. I can cite my own salad days as example, for I remember that very little was so worthy that it earned my respect, while a myriad of things were held in contempt. One of my favorite targets was the newspapers' advice columns; Dorothy Dix consoling a housewife whose husband left dirty laundry in the bedroom corner, or Ann Landers counseling a mother to ease up on the scoldings of her progeny. But occasionally, as I glanced at these columns, I began to see that in some cases this asking and giving of advice could actually be interesting, an opportunity to look into the lives of people which I could not find elsewhere. After a while I came to realize that from these letters I was learning about the ways of living by John Everyman and his wife Samantha, and finding it nearly as enlightening as in another column, that containing political and public and other information (which I, of course, had never mocked). To read the advice columns was like penetrating the walls of my neighbors, far and near, seeing an otherwise secluded, unavailable world: I was an invisible man sitting on multiple sofas watching how folks live.

Some time after that, I made another newspaper-related discovery: if the advice columns depicted the personal problems of the people and the news itself informed us of all information about the public stage, so the letters to the editor, which I had also superciliously ignored, provided me with a record of the thinking of the common people, of the opinions concerning national and international activity: I could learn what they thought about such complicated and complex topics as race, religion, sex, prejudice, politics, gays, and guns. Something like this was done when Thomas Jefferson, struggling with Alexander to make our country a democracy, not a monarchy, said he was willing to engage in a "newspaper contest" to help his cause. Of course he would not write letters, but in essence he would be doing what we do today, offering any interested reader knowledge of someone's thinking about important public matters. (The difference, obviously, being that Jefferson was also making news, while we may only read about it.)The people's letters, varying in quality and opinion and ability to convince, with numerous attempts to devastate the assertions of a previous missive, were not only informative of opinion but also on occasion revealing of character: we could better understand that group called the silent majority, silent no more.

I can't say I now read every letter in my local newspaper, but I look each day for topics that interest me, especially those which give opposing assertions, providing me with both entertainment (one can hardly believe some of the soberly inane pronouncements) and education (other letters are clear, well-written, informative). Eventually I found myself so put out by some of what I considered drivel that I got into the game, unable to allow such seeming idiocy to pass unopposed. I confess, of course, that ego was part of the inclination to write my own letters--I rather like seeing my name in print, even on a medical prescription--but I believe the stronger motive was to prevent some downright nonsense from going unanswered, perhaps influencing some readers who didn't know better. My reader here may see where I succeeded and where I failed, and may, I hope, learn some things about the beliefs of people concerning

1

national matters.

The following, then, are the letters I have had printed in the New Jersey Bergen Record, the Long Island Newsday, The New Yorker, the Yale Alumni Magazine and The New York Times (newspaper and book review), along with a few op-ed articles on subjects that needed room for explication or simply ideas and events I hoped to be of interest. I have lightly edited the letters and articles, finding a better word or making a sentence clearer, but have not in any place changed an opinion or taken advantage of information given since the letter was written. When it has seemed informative, I have added a comment, bringing an interesting issue up to date. And I must mention that *The Record* occasionally edits its letters; as they appear here, they are what I originally wrote, simply on the grounds that I prefer my version to theirs.

Format

The format is as follows:

1. "From:" paper name; date of letter to which I will reply. (In some cases, date not available).
2. "The argument:" summary of the letter to which I replied.
3. "From:" paper name; date of my reply.
4. "The reply."
5. My letter.
6. My name (in addition to my liking to see it in print, it marks the end of argument and reply, precedes beginning of next letters.)

I hope the reader will forgive such slips, omissions, and errors to be found in the following. The email work lacks the benefit of an editor.

Richard Lettis, Ph.D

1975, Newsday

From: *Newsday*, Op-Ed, September 7:

Lighting Our Children's Way.

Remember Prometheus?* He was a Titan who thought that man should have fire, and so stole it from the gods and gave it to humans. For that offense against divinities, the gods chained Prometheus to a rock and let vultures pluck at his entrails. A pretty stiff punishment.

Why were the gods so put out? What did giving fire mean? Fire is energy; it extends man's power beyond his mere animal muscle so that he can do things he never could have done as heatless anthropoid--go to the moon, for example. But more important, fire is light: it illuminates, makes things clear, helps us to see, to discover, to understand.

The English poet, William Blake, writing in the 18th century, was fascinated by the opposing views of Prometheus and his punishers. His poem "The Tyger" focusses upon the question in the opening lines:

Tiger! Tiger! Burning bright
In the forests of the night,
What immortal hand or eye
Could frame thy fear symmetry?

The voice of the poem suggests why the Greek gods got fussed: the tiger is fearful fire, terrible to look upon, ready to flame out and consume us while we stand mesmerized by his brilliance--all things only deities should have. Yet is there not a second voice in this and the rest of the poem, one perhaps rather felt than heard, which speaks for Prometheus? The tiger, though terrifying, is also strong, beautiful, and awesome. And what happens to us if the tiger fire goes out? We are left alone in forests belonging to darkness.

Who is right, then? Prometheus or his opposition? Those in terror of the tiger, or those who fear the forest? If we apply the question to our philosophy of education, I suppose initially we will all declare that we opt for fire, for lighting our children's way through the woods.

Who doesn't want their son or daughter to be educated, see and do, to understand? Why do so many overburdened parents give up their hard-earned dollars for college expenses? Why are parents devastated when a son drops out of school to get a job, and heartbroken if a daughter gives up a degree for a husband? We Americans believe in education, so much so that sometimes Europeans laugh at us for it. We aver that education makes good citizens, successful workers, prosperous and happy people.

Who is on the side of the dark forest? Nobody, in this enlightened age, should be. Of course there are some crannies and corners of knowledge we'd rather not have lighted up for our kids, some forest paths we'd just as soon prevent the burning tiger from illuminating, at least not too brightly, not too soon. Parents in Cold Spring Harbor recently, for example, have not seen the need for teaching their children if it means allowing a particular book in the local library which, if anybody read it, would convey information about the sexual practices that our American prisons force upon their inmates. And in other Long Island communities parents have been throwing cold water on the idea of sex education. Elsewhere in the country schools parent groups have differed over whether light should be permitted to shine on literature that is, in somebody's opinion, unpatriotic.

Such incidents are common. Perhaps no one has ever served a full term on a school-board in this country without encountering a group which insists that our kids be kept in the dark about sex, communism, hippie poetry, anti-war literature, information about drugs. Probably none of this can be construed as a desire to douse the tiger; it does seem, though, that many of us want to put him on a leash. Perhaps it is more honest to say that we don't want a flaming tiger-teacher at all; what we want is a poodle with a flashlight, and we want to tell it where to aim the beam. And if it points it elsewhere, if it rescues from the dark something that we find unsuitable, then out with the rock and the chains, and line up the buzzards.

Is there anything wrong with that? We place ourselves halfway between Prometheus and the gods; we are moderates; we have learned from Barry Goldwater that nothing fails like success. We're all for fire, up to a point. We want our kids to learn, but not learn too much. Teach the tots too much, and they may all want to go to the moon, or to Europe, or at least (unchaperoned) to Fort Lauderdale. Give them literature on sex and they may "get the wrong idea" (by which we mean of course the right one). Expose them to atheists or communists and they may become infected, and defect from those truths we once thought so self-evident.

It is difficult, it is frightening, to argue with such a position. Education is dangerous stuff, just about as dangerous as life. But before we assign our children to an education of selective illumination, perhaps we should face a few considerations. If we don't let them go where their tiger takes them, are we sure they will ever become anything like our hopes for them? If we don't allow access to information that may give them the wrong idea, will they ever have the chance to find the right one? If we are afraid that they will be confused or corrupted by sex or atheism or communism or anti-Americanism, how much can we hope they may ever know about love or God or democracy or the United States? Those who would limit (in the background lurks the darker word, censor) our children's education in essence tell us that kids are weak, unable to cope with so formidable an adversary as sex.

With Prometheus, as with Christ (another troublesome giver of

light), there is no middle position; ye are either for or against him.
Education is indeed a dangerous thing: if we give it to all out
children they may burn themselves, may turn on, drop out, refuse to be
drafted, join the Party. But one of Blake's fellow poets, Alexander
Pope, suggested that there is something even more dangerous than a lot
of learning. You may remember what it was†.

    Richard Lettis

    *The name means forethought.

    #One of the greatest founders of our country, Thomas Jefferson,
believed we could only become a successful democracy if we took all
good steps to educate the people. He was the main force in
establishing the University of Virginia.

    †"A little learning is a dangerous thing."

    (Censorship is, like death and taxes, always with us, but I felt
that it was especially dangerous at the time of this writing, and so
the reader will find more on the subject below. Since this article,
time has taught me that my letting a son lose a job but confining a
daughter to marriage is anti-PC, but I leave it in; no fair pretending
I was free of fault in those days.)

    (My reader may be interested to know that "The Tyger" was part of
a series called "Songs of Experience." Blake wrote another series,
"Songs of Innocence," in which a companion poem appeared; it was
called "The Lamb," and was of course totally opposite to the tiger:
helpless, simple, blessed. Probably almost everyone who likes poetry
has read "The Tyger"; "The Lamb" appears infrequently. Here are the
two poems.)

The Lamb

Little lamb, who made thee
Dost thou know who made thee?
Gave thee life and bid thee feed

Richard Lettis, Ph.D

By the stream and o'er the mead;
Gave thee clothing for delight,
Softest clothing lily bright;
Gave thee such a tender voice,
Making all the vales rejoice!
Little Lamb who made thee
Dost thou know who made thee?

Little lamb, I'll tell thee,
Little lamb, I'll tell thee!
He is called by thy name,
For he calls himself a lamb:
He is meek and he is mild,
He became a little child:
I a child and thou a lamb,
We are called by his name.
Little lamb God bless thee,
Little lamb God bless thee.

The Tyger
Tyger, tiger, burning bright,
In the forests of the night,
What immortal hand or eye,
Could frame thy fearful symmetry?

In what distant deep or skies
Burnt the fire of the eyes!
ON what wings dare he aspire?
What the hand, dare seize the fire?

And what shoulder, & what art
Could twist the sinews of thy heart?

And when thy heart began to beat,
What dread hand, and what dread feet?

What the hammer? What the chain,
In what furnace was thy brain?
What the anvil? What dread grasp,
Dare his deadly powers clasp?

When the stars threw down their spears
And water'd heaven with their tears:
Did he smile his work to see?
Did he who made the lamb make thee?

Tyger, tyger, burning bright
In the forests of the night,
What immortal hand or eye,
Dare frame thy fearful symmetry?)

Richard Lettis, Ph.D

1977, March 20th, Newsday

From: *Newsday*, Op-Ed, March 20:

The Book Is Not for Burning

Censorship has of late acquired such a bad reputation that it is almost impossible to practice it without first repudiating it. "I'm no censor," the would-be censor hotly argues, "but - - -." Despite our growing conviction that books should be consumed by eyes, not flames, there are still a few burning "buts" that need to be put out.

By far the most popular, successful, and unchallenged negative injunction now scorching our literature is the argument that children need to be protected. Perhaps few of us will be inflamed these days by the thought of adults wading through "filth", but who can keep their cool when they think of exposing kids to such stuff?

Such a book, the fiery censors of Long Island Tree's School Board have repeatedly argued, is J. D. Salinger's novel, "The Catcher in the Rye." It has foul language. One of its characters is a prostitute. It openly describes and discuses sexual perversion. Worst of all, it tells the story of a teenager, a boy with whom our children may identify, who does all sorts of objectionable things like drinking and dropping out of school and disobeying his parents and all. We're not censors, but obviously such things are not good for our children, and we object heatedly when we find that book in our school library.

The astonishing thing is that Holden Caulfield, the boy in the book, agrees with us. He's no censor, either, but he asserts with considerable warmth that certain words and ideas are dangerous for children and so should be erased. In one scene, for example, while searching for his beloved sister Phoebe, he sees the English-speaking world's classically bad four letter word written on the school wall, and angrily tries to rub it out, wishing for deep punishment of the writer.

Holden's desire to protect children from bad words is but a part of his conviction that they in all ways must be sheltered from an evil world. In thinking about what he himself would like to do as an adult, he imagines a huge field of rye in which thousands of children are playing. The field (childhood) is on the edge of a "crazy cliff" (corrupting adulthood), and the children in their play are in danger of falling off. Holden thinks he would like to be the one to save them: "I mean if they're running and they don't look where they're going I have to come out from somewhere and catch them. I'd just be the catcher in the rye . . ."

How can it be that that the protagonist of the story we all want to censor is himself a kind of censor? Why has Salinger put into his objectionable book an objectionable character who rejects the objectionable? The answer lies in what Holden later learns about "catching" children, in what he finds to be the cost of keeping them from possible harm. The "fall" they are in danger of taking is the inevitable departure from the garden of innocence, through experience, into the sordid city of adulthood. Like us, Holden dreads this terrible step, for he sees the adult world as a shabby and corrupting place. But he comes to realize that there is only one method for preventing children from taking this fall, only one way to catch them. Only one child in Holden's story will never be contaminated by adulthood: his other beloved sibling, Allie. Allie is dead.

To be the catcher in the rye, one has to be a kind of killer; there is no other way to keep children from growing into a corrupting adulthood. The alternative to a life in a dangerous and sordid world is no life at all (we think of Hamlet's great question). When Holden has come to understand this, he takes Phoebe for a ride on a carousel, and watches her reaching for the gold ring. Though he is afraid she may fall and injure herself, he decides that he must not try to stop her. It is not that Holden becomes less concerned for children, or

11

less anguished by their fall. It is simply that he has come to understand the alternative.

When children reach out for the golden ring, it is time for them to get off the merry-go-round; even if they do so by a fall; we have to let them do it. When children are ready to encounter the larger world of adult experience, we must not inhibit them, no matter how much it hurts to watch the hurt. To the extent that we do prevent them, we prevent them from growing--that is, living.

One of the surest ways of growing is to read. But often it is that very kind of reading which makes us more fearful for the welfare of our children--reading about controversial things like violence and rejection of traditional values, reading about sex---which will do the most to help them grow. The "safe" books in the library, of which we comfortably approve, are frequently the ones which keep young minds on the merry-go-round, moving only in a circle, repeating the same limited values and simplified concepts which were right for their childish comprehension but are insufficient for, and even damaging to, their expanding intellects.

The point is not that children should be steeped in sex, inundated with immorality or pressed to abandon their early beliefs. But if the convictions a youngster has been given are to become truly his, he must make them so by refining, modifying, developing, and testing them. To do this, the child must read books which are sometimes troublesome, challenging, controversial, argumentative.

The child who reaches for the ring of gold may wind up with brass, or worse. He may adopt wrong ideas, acquire reprehensible tastes, become confirmed in immoral behavior, develop a way of life that is repugnant to us. But that is the chance that we and our child have to take. While he or she was a child, we gave all we could to help him and her choose well, a sense of our concept of right, a sense of their own dignity, a sense of mutual love. We can still advise them, urge our way of life upon them, love them. But we must not keep them from reaching out. When they do, they will inevitably and perhaps fortunately fall, and we must steel ourselves not to catch. It should not be too difficult to refrain, not if we remember the alternative of the fall.

Richard Lettis

Richard Lettis, Ph.D

1978, March 5th, Newsday

From: *Newsday*, Op-Ed, March 5:

"When TV Keeps Young People from Growing Up"

I see by the papers where the National PTA has decided that the Osmond show is "good" television, while a situation comedy dealing with adult themes is "bad."

As Star Trek's Mr. Spock always said when something particularly outlandish or plain dumb happened on the Enterprise, "fascinating." The definition of good and bad exhibited by these PTA preferences gives us compelling insight into the minds of contemporary American parents. What do we see there?

The Osmonds are "wholesome . . . bright and positive," the PTA tells us, inspired no doubt by Donny and Marie's gleaming teeth, while "Maude" is disgusting and "almost vulgar"--comments probably prompted by the mammary development of the actress Adrienne Barbeau. Whether or not it's teeth vs. breasts (one must sacrifice alliteration to propriety) they have in mind, the parents obviously like the Osmonds because they are good clean fun, and object to the Maudes because they are bad dirty fun--to boil it down to the grits, because one show is sexless and devoid of social complications and the other is not. What we see, then, is organized parentdom, once again struggling, like Sisyphus with his stone, to protect the child from what no one can protect.

In choosing between Marie and Maude, the PTA reiterates the American desire to keep young people away from the one thing they should not and cannot be prevented from reading. It exposes the parental conviction that children should not grow up. It restates its desire that they watch mush rather than view matter, chew gum rather than take in food, sit mindless before glittering emptiness rather than encounter the tarnished but vital materials of human existence.

I hope I'm not misunderstood: "Maude" is not one of western culture's better examinations of the nature of things; compared to the average good novel published this year it is slight stuff. But by contrast with devastating dentures and dainty dialogue and silly songs, it at least deals with something like life as we know it, and invites us to respond, to feel something about, even ponder, that life. That, of course, is exactly why some parents don't like it.

The strong sexual overtones the PTA finds in "Maude" (about as strong as small beer, if you compare them with the hard liquor of sexuality in Shakespeare or D. H. Lawrence or the Bible) are dangerous because they invite the viewer to become aware of such things as physical desire in and out of wedlock, some of the difficulties that may be engendered by such desire, and even an occasional so-called aberrant sexual practice. Why is it that most parents would rather have their children's minds massaged into vacuity by meaningless entertainment than allow them to confront such things? I think the answer is found in that fear which is so dominant in our adult world. Parents are so frightened by what they have lived through--though usually they have done so with some creditable degree of strength and courage and conviction--that they are terrified of allowing their children to begin to live too.

Better to have Junior permanently arrested in his playroom than let him know that some men cheat on their wives, better to keep Sis forever fixed on her denatured dolls than expose her to the frightening force of sexuality. When Junior grows up and is astonished to find that interest in other women does not end with the marriage contract, when Sis meets the first male who tempts her to do what mommy and daddy would never discuss but hinted she must never do, neither will have anything to fall back on as they try to understand what's happening to them.

But no matter: the time for that is far in the future, and for now the kids won't get dirty if they're kept from dirty shows. Children no longer need the blood of the Lamb to wash away impurities, because we keep them forever sanitized. Well, not for ever. Just until it's too late to help.

"A healthy mind cannot be contaminated by words which are not so proper," a writer named Boccaccio once said. He might have added that a healthy mind can become stunted if it is limited to words and ideas that are everlastingly and relentlessly decorous. It can be starved by a diet of "wholesomeness" and "bright" baby foods, that give it insufficient substance, and no roughage, and if it survives the Pablum diet it is sure to be undone by the first solid steak it is given to chew on.

The parents who protest the loudest against questionable programs and objectionable movies and dirty books are the same people who wonder why there are so many premarital pregnancies and devastating divorces and ugly sex crimes, and try to blame it all on the very things they have prevented their children from seeing. How painfully ironic to find one of our country's prominent educational associations joining in such erroneous and destructive judgment.

Richard Lettis

1979, October 1st, Newsday

From: *Newsday*, Op-Ed, October 1:

"To Pay--Or Not to Work"

In a few weeks I expect to be confronted with an unpleasant choice: whether to lose the teaching position I have held for nearly 20 years and throw myself into an overcrowded job market, or make a payment of $612 in back fees to an organization of which I disapprove.

Eight of my colleagues and I have been informed by our college's faculty union (the C. W. Post Collegial Federation) and by the National Labor Relations Board that we must either act against our sincerely-held convictions or give up our life's work.

Whether we are right or wrong in our disagreement with the union is arguable, but whether we or any person in a free society should be forced to support that in which they do not believe seems to me not subject to debate.

Some of my best friends and most respected colleagues are members of the union, and I would not imply that it is comparable to bodies that are regarded by good men and women everywhere as evil. But perhaps to convey a sense of how I feel about what I soon may have to do, I must draw some such comparison.

Those who hated the Vietnam War, yet found their taxes supporting it, those who consider capital punishment to be a crime, yet are obliged to pay for it, those who have sums deducted from their pay to help politicians they dislike get elected--perhaps only people with such experience can fully comprehend the outrage I feel at being obliged to contribute to an organization which I sincerely oppose.

In choosing my comparisons, I have wittingly offered a line of argument to those on the other side: such things happen all the time; in a large society nobody can be guaranteed perfect freedom of

conscience; life puts pressure on all of us. Admittedly, I am biased
by my situation, but I think it is a poor line of argument. I'm
compelled to think that there are few evils worse than forcing a man
to do that which he believes to be wrong.

I know it is argued that we are not really forced: we may be
pressed, but we do have a choice. I cannot speak for my colleagues,
but there is no choice for me: the subsistence of others depends on my
salary, and I may not sacrifice their livelihood to my convictions.

I draw some consolation from the fact that our society has
obliged relatively few people to dishonor themselves publicly as I
must do. If I could think of myself as among the last to be so
disgraced, I might even capitulate without bitterness of heart. But a
number of people I have talked to seem to think I am making a pretty
big fuss about a rather small matter. And so I am not just bitter: I
am afraid.

Richard Lettis

(This is my first published letter. I did feel strongly about
teachers' unions, and I thought then that the overwriting was pretty
impressive. And I dealt rather too simply with a troublesome and
complex problem; if we had to get every citizen to agree to something
before we could do it, we would have zero activity. And college
faculties waited a long and hard time, with inadequate pay ("they
should be happy to teach, and not be money-grubbers") before they fell
back on an organization which could improve their job. But the union
also deprives students of their (because of strikes) classes, which
they paid for and need: I simply could not support something that
would wipe out the first weeks of my classes' semester. Fairness
requires that I mention that the union did not force me to pay,
perhaps because I had been a part of Post College for some time. My
letter should have recognized the complexity of the situation more
fully, and should have made it clear that I was not opposed to all
unions in all occupations.)

(N.B.: As I write this the Supreme Court is weighing the question of whether unions have the right to force members to pay dues.)

Richard Lettis, Ph.D

1979, October 28th, New York Times Magazine

From: *The New York Times Magazine*, October 28:

"The Pope, Rahner, and Christianity."

Comment:

So much of Karl Rahner's thought (in "Quiet Mover of the Catholic church," by Eugene Kennedy, Sept. 23) gives reason for rejoicing that it must seem graceless to find points on which to quibble. Yet two statements by the great theologian must be protested, for they perpetuate one of the great wrongs of Roman Catholicism, if not all Christian thought.

Dr. Rahner uses the term "Anonymous Christian" for people who possess "genuine religious spirit even though they might profess other faiths, or, seemingly, no faith at all." And he argues that "things that are humane are basically Christian." Are not both statements oppressive in their egotism? Does not Dr. Rahner reverse concentric circles, making the smaller (Christianity) the larger, and the larger (religious spirit, the humane) the smaller? Instead of reducing the world to his faith, might he not better fit his faith into the world?

Richard Lettis

(I recall an incident that occurred in Texas some years ago. A Protestant church burned down, and the local rabbi offered the basement of his synagogue for the congregation's worship. The minister thanked him and added, "It's a very Christian thing for you to do." The rabbi replied, "It is also a very Jewish thing for me to do." I think it possible that this kind of self-congratulation has helped fuel the incipient movement away from religion (which has always had its opponents, viz. Voltaire and Jefferson.)

1980, November 23rd, The New York Times

From: *The New York Times*, November:

The argument: (summarized) Hunting is merciful. It saves deer from starvation and disease.

From: *The New York Times*, November 23:

The reply:

For years I have resisted the thesis that hunting is humane, my argument being that what happens to animals is not as important as what goes on in the minds of men (and women?) who perpetuate the love of killing. But George Leahy (in "The Middle Road; Hunters with Consciences") has at last convinced me.

"Is it more humane than shooting deer," Mr. Leahy asks, "to let nature take its toll through starvation and disease? Having seen photographs of blind and tumored deer, I seriously doubt it."

Okay, merciful hunters, you win. But why not extend your compassion to people? In many areas of our country, humans are left to die in similar ways, and no one takes pity on them. Is it more humane to let nature take its toll through starvation and disease than to send dedicated gunmen into poverty-stricken regions and reduce the suffering by blazing away at anything that looks unhealthy? Having seen photographs of blind and tumored people , . . .

Richard Lettis

Richard Lettis, Ph.D

1980, May 31st, The New York Times

From: *The New York Times,* May 31 (article):
Isn't It Still a Prejudice If It's a Tiny One?
All right-thinking men and women are agreed upon the evil effects
of a great prejudice, but I wonder if even the wisest of us gives
sufficient attention and concern to the consequences of little ones.

By great prejudice I mean of course the national, sexual and
racial kinds: the unsubstantiated conviction that an Irishman must
drink heavily and lose his temper easily; that a woman must be passive
and inclined to hysteria; that a black must, as Gore Vidal put it,
have white teeth and a natural sense of rhythm but fail to phone in
when he can't come to work. Like huge animals, these great prejudices
are dangerous indeed, but their size alerts us to their threat, and we
can fortify our minds and hearts against them.

By little prejudices I refer to those lesser, unwarranted
assumptions we make about our neighbor, not on the basis of his or her
location in the phylum of sex or the classification of race, but by
identification with smaller groups — the genus of work, perhaps, or a
species of dress and physical appearance. Few civil rights groups
direct our attention to such things, and so our conscience is free to
put him in a pigeonhole marked "wise," or "stupid," "good" or "bad,"
worthy of our company or not, never again giving him that long and
careful study the least of these our brethren deserves before he is
fixed with a formulated phrase.

Whenever I think about such things, I remember something that
happened to me some years ago. I was at the time a fairly young
English teacher, making my way across the C. W. Post College campus to
conduct a summer class in composition. It was a bright, clear day, and
I was in no hurry to get out of nature and into my profession.

As I walked, I observed some construction men clearing ground for what was to be our new auditorium, and I ambled over to watch them at their labor. My path in the direction of one worker who, I noticed, was leaning on a shovel, looking at something on the newly cleared ground. He was a short thickly built man, with a coarse, heavy countenance; a casting director could not have found the face and body better suited to his station in life.

But something in his manner of staring at the ground seemed out of character: I walked a bit nearer, and saw that he was looking at a squirrel, which was half-sitting and half-lying on the bare earth and looking back at the worker at least as intently as he was regarding it. I was curious about the silent and motionless confrontation, but too shy or snooty or something to speak to a man so far removed from my own restricted sphere; I prepared to pass by on the other side.

"It's a damn shame," I heard the man say, in a manner suggesting that he, too, was reluctant to speak but had no choice. "Somebody oughta do sump'n about it." It was not clear that he was speaking to me, but there was no one else around and it seemed impolite to go on without responding. I summoned my scholarly eloquence. "What?" I said.

"It's a damn shame," the worker said. "We just cut down the tree, and he was in it. Broke his back in the fall. Somebody oughta do sump'n about it."

We stood together for a moment in silence while I read an essay in his last sentence. The first paragraph was on mercy: he felt compassion for the crippled animal before us. The second expressed helplessness: despite his crude pronunciation and rough clothes and rather brutish appearance, he found himself unable to end the animal's suffering by killing it. The third, I feared, was importunate: though he had said "somebody," I felt he had a particular body in mind. I looked around hopefully, but there was no other someone nearby.

Physically I am not the personification of Mr. Chips, but I do have about me something of the academic man — something of that quality that may be labeled, according viewer's angle of vision, cultivated, refined, sensitive, delicate, bookish, effete or sissified. I am perhaps not the last person on earth one would urge to kill something, but I am near the end of the line.

My worker, on the other hand, was quite clearly facing the other way, near the other end of the line — if not with the mark of Cain upon his brow, certainly with a look of readiness to bash anything or anybody that seemed in his judgment to require bashing. Yet here he stood, shovel in hand, looking at the suffering squirrel. And here I stood.

By now that composition class was waiting for me. I tried to find words to explain this to the workman, and failed. Instead, he found words.

"Yeah," he said. "Somebody oughta do sump'n about it."

Whatever my appearance, I am not so kind a soul as Sterne's Uncle Toby, who once chased a fly around his room, caught it, and gently let it out at window. I have slaughtered flies in my time, laid waste to hosts of mosquitoes and cockroaches. (On the other hand, I once, as a child, shied rocks at a frog in a pond, never dreaming of hitting it, and to my dismay did: the floating corpse haunted my waking dreams for years.)

Now I looked at the disabled squirrel and tried to recall everything I had ever heard against euthanasia, and could remember nothing. I saw the hindquarters lying helpless, twisted at an odd angle from the rest of the body. I saw the front legs braced, the face turned toward us in readiness for assault. I saw the bared teeth, the fierce expression, and was somehow reminded that, for all their pretty fur and fluffy tails and aerial habits, squirrels are just like rodents, like the rats we set traps for in our cellars. But then, this wasn't a cellar.

I felt much as Jonah must have felt when called upon by Yahweh. Oh cursed spite. Reluctantly I put my books down on a tuft of grass the workers had missed. The man beside me did not move, but I fancied that he had shifted the shovel slightly so that if I wished, I could have taken it from him more conveniently.

I did not wish, but I took it and stepped toward the squirrel. Convinced that I meant him no good, the broken fellow attempted to back off, keeping his teeth bared at me. Trying to act before I could think, and failing miserably, I held the shovel behind me, slung it up over my shoulder like a man chopping a log, and brought the flat blade down on the small body as hard as I could.

The squirrel seemed to leap from the ground almost as high as my heart leapt within my chest; then he fell to the earth and lay still.

"O.K., that does it," the worker said. He seized the shovel from my hands and began busily to dig a small hole in the earth. It occurred to me that I might have only stunned the animal, that he might now be buried alive; I voiced my concern.

"Naw, naw, it's O.K. that's done it," the worker said hurriedly, not looking at me (he never had), still shoveling hastily.

I picked up my books and walked away, no longer casually: I had a class to get to. I looked back once, just in time to see him scoop up the corpse I had made and drop it into the makeshift grave. He started to smooth the rough dirt over the spot, but I looked away. I had that class to get to.

That, as I say, was years ago, but often when I begin thinking about what I am and what other people are, I find myself remembering it. And when I do, I can never decide whether, at least at that moment, my worker and I were more like each other or more unlike. Which of us, for instance, would you say was the more sensitive? Which the more humane? Which with more resolve, which with less? Or were we equal, do you think, on all counts? I cannot say.

I do not mean to overdo this. Of course, my doubts are pretty much confined to that one moment we shared. As for other times and places, I feel fairly confident that I could name differences between us clearly and definitely. For example: although I have never forgotten my worker or squirrel during the years since that day, I daresay that from the moment we left his sight the worker never thought of either of us again. But perhaps I am wrong; perhaps he has.

Richard Lettis

1984, January 15th, New York Times

From: *The New York Times*, January 15:

The argument (summarized):

(I have tried every known way of retrieving my letter, but to no avail. I enclose the following disagreement, which gives some idea of the contents of the letter, and is worth reading. I do believe that the letter made several good points, and that Ms. Bernstein's dispute is limited to this one sentence.)

In his article ''Yes, That's Censorship'' (Opinion Page, Jan. 15), Richard Lettis distinguishes between removing books from school libraries and selecting them, claiming that ''when a teacher or librarian picks a book from among the countless texts available, he or she is not engaged in the act of censorship, but simply of selection.'' Not so simply.

Censors are endlessly creative and often do not wait until a book is purchased to demand its suppression. Legislators and textbook committees in several states have passed laws banning the purchase of books that deal with whole subject areas. Rather than have to remove them, the censors simply don't allow them to be selected. Like the old Southern law that once subjected a black man to a charge of rape if he looked menacingly at a white woman, the censor asks, ''Why wait till the last minute?''

Here is what has happened:

- In Oregon, the State Legislature, in a bill now under challenge by the A.C.L.U., ruled that no textbook could be used in the public schools that ''speaks slightingly of the founders of the republic or of those who preserved the union or which belittles or undervalues their work.''

- In Texas, the State Textbook Committee just rejected a rule that would have required the teaching of Darwin and evolution in any biology textbook. That is, though not banned outright, no discussion of evolution is required. The net effect is that creationism wins in Texas.

- In Hawaii and New Hampshire, school boards have defunded entire programs dealing with sex education and drug and alcohol abuse prevention.

- In California, two elementary textbooks in statewide use were sent back to the publisher to remove two pictures of a boy and a girl that a censorship group thought were insufficiently clothed.

- Again in California and in New Mexico, hundreds of copies of dictionaries were returned because of ''obscene'' words.

Nor is censorship only an act of removal, as Mr. Lettis claims. Censorship occurs when state lawmakers require that biology teachers bend their interpretation of the origins of the earth to include the biblical account. The fact that the Arkansas creationism bill was declared unconstitutional in an A.C.L.U. challenge has not prevented the Louisiana legislature from passing the same law, now also under challenge.

Much as we tend to think of censorship as a single parent marching through the library door to attack a particular book, more toxic to the First Amendment is the law that bans the idea behind the book and allows the censor to avoid a messy public confrontation because the book is not even there to oppose.

BARBARA BERNSTEIN Executive Director, Nassau County Chapter.

No reply:

(Perhaps Ms. Bernstein would have accepted my letter had I put the word "necessarily" before "engaged.")

1986, November 2nd, New York Times

From: *The New York Times*, Op-Ed, November 2:

The Darkling Season Brings a Fire to the Soul*

Among the several things I would do better than the Deity, if I could replace Him and do anything, would be the minor improvement of making leaves so that we could burn them without polluting the environment. My divine reform would not guarantee world peace, cure cancer, or even alleviate the pip, but it would restore to American life one of the little gratifications of autumn.

When I was a child, I endured the September return to school's compulsions with just a bit more composure because I knew that in a month or two my father would begin to transform our lawn from red and yellow and brown back to green again, pulling the leaves into the gutter in a long, high-piled row.

These leaves were not Shelley's dead thoughts, aimed at quickening the universe; they were the quintessential stuff for scuffing, they were a play mound into which one could leap and virtually disappear, and they were fuel for the most delightful fire a child can know. I think that burning leaves made a child again of my father, as remembering it now makes me one once more.

My dad would not light the leaves all at once by walking along the row and setting it ablaze in several places so that the pile would burn up quickly. Instead, he would apply his match at just one end, allowing me to watch the progress of the fire through the long narrow pile, seeing it flame out with warmth and beauty where the leaves were dry, and smolder beneath the surface when they were damp, sending up the lovely curling blue smoke that we were too innocent to suspect of the evil we now know of, and sending forth one of the world's most enchanting fragrances.

Richard Lettis, Ph.D

I love life's evocative aromas, but I think that none--not even the interior of a brand-new auto, nor frying bacon, nor perfume from a dress--quite meets the heart's olfactory desire like the thick, thrusting smell of burning leaves.

Sometimes the fire would go out, and my father would have to relight it, but this always seemed a bit like cheating, and we would wait a long time before descending to such degrading compromise, anxiously watching the place in the leaves where the last dying ember had been seen. And often our patience would be rewarded by a tendril of smoke snaking up like the beginning of Jack's beanstalk, a portent this time not of giants and gold in the sky but of our little conflagration still alive below.

And if we gazed long enough, and sometimes--again with a slight sense of unfairly forcing the issue--helped out by blowing on the hopeful spot, flame would flicker up once more, and perhaps a whole clump of dry leaves would catch with a little roar, and the fire would resume its advance down the long waiting row.

What we had at the end, of course, was a valley of ashes, almost as dead and troublesome as that in Fitzgerald's *The Great Gatsby*. But I always took comfort in thinking that rain would within a week or so wash the gutter clean, and all that would be left was the memory, which with a Wordsworthian beneficence clung to me as the smell of burning leaves remained in my outdoor clothes. Would that the odor held me still, as does the memory.

Yes, the smoke adhered to my lungs, too, and to the lungs of people who perhaps took no delight in burning leaves but were obliged to suffer for my pleasure, a price too high to pay. But what a pity it is. For a day each fall, my father and I transmuted the dull reality of our gutter into an Eden for sight and senses.

If I could make the choice for myself alone, who knows but I might elect to go back again to see and smell the burning leaves, even though now I recognize the inseparable serpent.

*This luscious title was provided by the editor; I am both pleased and a little doubtful, wondering if my soul was really involved.

(I wrote this a long time ago, and hadn't read it again for years. I find it has helped me to recall other pleasantly emotional incidents, mainly of my childhood but of some later times as well. I like to think that reading it may awaken others to moments in their lives the memories of which could enrich the past.)

Richard Lettis, Ph.D

1989, December, New York Times

From: *The New York Times*, December:

Content: Novelists list great works they dislike.

From: *The New York Times,* January 1:

Comment:

To the Editor:

Your symposium on great books disliked by contemporary writers, in addition to demonstrating once again that some people simply cannot respond to questions put to them, reminds me of a college test I once heard of. At the end of a course on the English novel, the students were given a final that contained just two questions.

The first, on the first sheet, was, ''Which novel read this semester did you dislike the most?''

The second, on the second page, was, ''To what deficiencies in your intellect and character do you attribute this dislike?''

Richard Lettis

(Sounds like a tale--how would the professor grade the tests?-- but does make the point.)

1994, December 12th, New York Times

From: *The New York Times*, December 12:

Argument: "Old Clichés" are of use.

From: *The New York Times*, January 24:

The reply:

We must all be really and truly grateful for the advice in a recent Book Review headline, "Haul Out the Old Clichés" (Dec. 12), for it is certainly true and not false that they are much better than the new ones. And while we're all at it, let's see if we can haul out some of those old editors who used to check sentences before they got into print, and from time to time deleted infelicitous phrases like, oh, say, repetitive redundancies.

Richard Lettis

(Unnecessary adjectives ("dead corpse," "rich millionaire," "little dwarf") are not the worst fault in writing, but brevity has always been important, and one expects such a publication as *The New York Times* to have good writing (all clichés, of course, are old). It is interesting that concise writing may take longer to compose than one of length: a man once wrote a lengthy missive to a friend and said, "Please excuse this long letter; I haven't time to be brief.")

Richard Lettis, Ph.D

1996, June 17th, The New Yorker

From: *The New Yorker*, June 17:

Subject: Description of anti-Semitism in T.S. Eliot.

From: *The New Yorker*, June 24:

Comment:

The article on Anthony Julius's views about T. S. Eliot's anti-Semitism reminded me of some of the critical reaction to Charles Dickens's anti-Semitic writing. As with Eliot, the bigotry was at first both ignored and then vigorously denied by apologists. But as more evidence was revealed (e.g. in Dickens's unexpurgated letters), Dickensians began to accept the fact that Dickens did, indeed, hate Jews (at least until the later years of his life). But Dickens's readers, unlike Julius, did not decide that "an anti-Semite is a scoundrel." Perhaps this was because Dickens seemed to be so great as to be irreproachable; perhaps it was simply because they couldn't bring themselves to condemn someone they so loved. Or perhaps it was because they thought it took more than a single conviction, even one so devastatingly wrongheaded and damaging, to make a person a scoundrel. They seem to have decided that Dickens was a man of his time and, like the rest of us, was cursed with flaws we wish we and he didn't have.

Richard Lettis

1996, October 22nd, New York Times

From: *The New York Times*, Op-Ed, October 22:

Because, like more and more Americans, my wife and I love dining out, and love it most where we find those three requirements of a good restaurant (good food, good ambiance, and good service), we used to seek out as often as we could the wonderful restaurants in New York City.

But because of the long drive on the Long Island Expressway (termed the world's longest parking lot), the higher cost for dinner, and the long wait in a parking garage to get our car (also at an ugly penny), we now have scaled down to some of the local restaurants, and have found that with careful selection we can eat just about as well: Long Island has its share of superior restaurants, in which meals rivaling the better New York establishments are offered for fewer fifties and in pleasant surroundings and with efficient service.

But that service, though usually competent, has on occasion its problems (granted, New York occasionally has some too). Too often in a fine restaurant with delightful decor and delectable dinner, we have been served by a waiter who has forgotten, or never learned, the refinements of his art.

Why will a restaurateur surround his fare with costly furniture, dinnerware and tablecloths, only to mar the scene with a waiter who greets his customers with ''How ya doin', folks?'' It's like slapping supermarket mustard on a sirloin.

I don't know if there is a waiters' school on Long Island, but there should be. In my experience, most Long Island waiters need no training to be prompt, or pleasant, or efficient, but beyond these essentials much remains to be learned if the diner is to be greeted with tact, seated easily, helped with the order, served, assisted in

35

paying, and ushered out

When I dine out, I want all things to be smooth and easy; a jarring note can hurt the evening, the waiter's tip, and the restaurant's chance of seeing me again. If I were an instructor in a waiter's school, I would make the following points:

To start, ''How ya doin'?'' is a poor start. In addition to the unpleasant pronunciation, the question means nothing, seems to require an answer but really desires and certainly elicits no sensible response, and makes the diner think he is in a diner, not a restaurant.

Disturbing too is the waiter who gives us his name and announces the fact we rather suspected on our own: he is our waiter tonight. I assume the intention is to make it all friendly, personal, homey, but I don't care what his name is, and we did not come to establish a long friendship. When I sit at a restaurant table, I don't want a dialogue, I want service.

Once seated, we should not find ourselves waiting for the waiter. If busy, the host(ess) should see that we are occupied until he can come: a busboy will fill glasses, bring bread and remove unneeded plates, and a barmaid should ask if we would like a drink. A good restaurant has the sense to hire enough waiters, and though I recognize problems may arise in getting them, I don't want to go to a place that regularly requires me to take along, well, "War and Peace."

Most waiters I have had do well in taking orders. They describe dishes, convey no sense of urgency, and do not pretend to be my lodge brother. The first of these items is most important: no waiter should be ignorant of the ingredients or preparation of any dish on the menu, and an ''I'll have to check'' is a confession of incompetence, while ''Would you like me to find out?'' is unforgivable: if I wouldn't like, I wouldn't have asked.

Still worse: In some good restaurants we have found waiters who seize this time to push food upon their customers. I can read the menu, and if I want an appetizer, I will ask for it: ''No soup or vegetable?'' implies that, idiot that I am, I have forgotten a course no true diner should be without, and leaves me with the impression that my waiter wants a bigger bill, for a bigger tip. He'll get a smaller one.

I am annoyed by the waiter who, especially at a table for two (have I written a song lyric?), cannot remember who ordered what. Holding two entrees, he waves both before us, with a question ranging from the most objectionable ''Who gets the chopped liver?'' to the better but still unacceptable ''Prime rib?''

I know that, while we are dining, the waiter's appearing with an ''Everything all right here?'' or some such expression is intended to express a laudable concern, but truly, I could do without it. Better for him to keep an eye on me and my partner, and promptly come if we signal. (I have sometimes been asked how the food is before I had the chance to begin eating it.)

I have respect for waiters. Theirs is a demanding business and they work hard. But the truly good waiter never lets me see how busy he is. He does not rush to or from my table or wear a harried expression. He also does whatever is necessary to control perspiration: a whiff of body odor really takes the savor out of the best meal.

One thing waiters in even the best Long Island restaurants seem not to have been taught is to clear the plates of all diners at the table at the same time. This is partly due, I think, to the mistaken notion that pouncing at the first sign of possible service is a mark of good waiting. It is not.

A plate should stay in front of a diner until all at the table have finished; then the quick and efficient removal should begin. The competent diner will, when finished, put fork and knife on his plate, and the good waiter will know of and recognize this signal. When in doubt whether all have completed their meals, the waiter should of course ask, but never by saying, ''All done?'' which sounds to my ear like Mommy's question in my toilet-training days. ''Finished?'' is a little better, but not much: the best inquiry I have heard was in a nice little restaurant in Key West, in which the waiter asked, ''May I clear?'' If I were a restaurateur, I would have all my waiters use that phrase.

It is my experience that the hardest time to get a waiter's attention is when the meal is finished. He warms my neck with his breath throughout the evening, but when I am ready for the check, he appears to have decided to take up another line of work.

Are these fussy, finicky points? I don't think so. A truly good dining experience is an artistic performance, from chef to busboy (who, in passing, really does not need to fill my water glass when it is already three-quarters full; he is impressing his supervisor, not me).

The restaurant I go back to repeatedly is of course the one with delicious food and lovely appointments; but it is also the restaurant in which the waiter hones his performance to the same sharpness achieved by all the other members of the troupe. For him my gratuity is generous, and really is an expression of thanks.

Richard Lettis

(A subsequent letter following this article accused me of the fussiness I had said I did not think I had; the lady expressed special contempt for my potty-training comment, suggesting some infantile fixation. She may have been right in part--I now wince at some of the judgments--but I still think on the whole I had some good advice.)

1998, May 4th, New York Times

From: *The New York Times*, Metropolitan Diary, May 4:

Call It a Day

Monday is the bad day: back to the dull grind;

Tuesday is a better day: Monday is behind;

Wednesday is a hopeful day; week is halfway through;

Thursday is a ho-hum day: nothing much to do;

Friday is a good day: weekend's here at last;

Saturday and Sunday,

Each can be a fun day,

Though we know what's on the way:

Monday.

Richard Lettis

Richard Lettis, Ph.D

1998, September 7th, New York Times

From: *The New York Times*, September 7:

To the Sports Editor:

One of the most interesting things about Mark McGwire's and Sammy Sosas's march to fame is the ovations they have received in every ball park they have played in. This phenomenon has been understandably criticized by some who argue that true fans should not root against their own teams, but if my experience is typical, that is not quite what has been done.

A friend and I watched McGwire hit Nos. 50 and 51 in a doubleheader at Shea Stadium, and though we were pulling hard for the Mets, and felt sorry for the two pitchers involved, there was simply no way we could regret watching a mighty slugger (and very nice guy) move two homers closer to his great goal. I think the feeling in the park was, ''Let's cheer him if he hits one, and then hope for our guys to win.'' In each of the two games, he did, and we cheered; in one of the two, they did, and we all cheered that, too.

Richard Lettis

(The two mentioned players were both attempting to break Hank Aaron's record for home runs. McGuire made it, but the happy story is marred by the subsequent discovery that he was using performance-enhancing drugs, a problem for baseball at least through the 2004 season, when the Yankees' Alex Rodriguez was suspended for the offense.)

2001, September 27th, New York Times

From: *The New York Times Book Review*, September 27:

To the Editor:

Charles McGrath writes a fine review of ''Boswell's Presumptuous Task,'' Adam Sisman's book on Boswell and Johnson (Aug. 19), but he misses the wit of their first meeting and exchange. Boswell did, as McGrath says, apologize for being Scottish, but it was his saying ''I do indeed come from Scotland, but I cannot help it'' that gave Johnson the opening for his barbed reply: his ''That, Sir, I find, is what a very great many of your countrymen cannot help'' is directed not at Boswell's nationality but at his and his countrymen's ''coming from'' Scotland to pester the people of London. Thus began the long and fascinating dialogue that Boswell's book records.

Richard Lettis

(Samuel Johnson was a great literary figure in the eighteenth century, perhaps rather more for his place and character and beliefs than for his writing. That was prolific--he wrote a novel, poetry, edited a journal, and produced what is considered the first full dictionary--but is now known chiefly for his friendship with James Boswell, who also initiated a new genre, a biography, which was of his good friend. The above conversation was caused by the fact that Johnson held strong opinions, including a prejudice against Scotland; Boswell was, of course, Scottish.)

Richard Lettis, Ph.D

2003, February 17th, New York Times

From: *The New York Times*, Article, February 17:

Riding to the city on the Long Island Rail Road, I was challenged by the conductor concerning my senior ticket, good for those 65 and older. Of course I felt flattered.

''Is 74 old enough?'' I asked.

''Well,'' he said, ''I've got to test you.''

''You want my birth year?''

''No, I'm too dumb to figure that out. Let's see -- uh -- what shaving cream company used to advertise by placing poems on small signs along the road?''

''Burma Shave,'' I said.

''O.K., you pass.''

''Every Sheba wants a sheik,'' I went on from faulty memory, ''strong of arm and clean of cheek. Burma Shave.''

Not quite right, as it turned out, but close enough to impress the conductor.

''Ah, you're too much for me,'' he said, and moved on.

I do not always enjoy my trips on the L.I.R.R., but this time I did.

Richard Lettis

(The Long Island railroad had a less than admirable reputation back then, with trains running late, sometimes lacking heat in winter and air conditioning in summer. An example of inefficiency is an incident suffered by me and a friend as we took the train from Port Washington to the Mets' Shea Stadium for a ball game. As we approached the station, the train did not slow down, and soon we heard a voice explaining that the conductor had forgotten to stop at the station. Julian and I had to get off at the next stop and pay for a ride back to the stadium, barely making it in time for the first pitch. The fact that not all trains stop at that station is one small excuse, but we were then in no mood to forgive. All of this made Burma Shave a happy exception, I no longer live on Long island so cannot say whether the railroad has improved.)

2006, January 27th, The Record

From: *The Record*, January 23:

Argument: The writer applauds the fact that "The Book of Daniel" has been forcibly removed from television.

From: *The Record*, January 27:

The reply:

I am sad to learn that the American Family Association — which no doubt is presently saying, "we're not censors, but . . ." — has succeeded in forcing "The Book of Daniel" off the TV screen, claiming as it's right the power to decide what the rest of us may and may not see.

Jesus forgave those who tortured him to death. But these Christians cannot abide the few representations of contemporary life that the program offers, demonstrating yet once again that for the far right, religion's primary principle is "Thou shalt not."

Richard Lettis

(*The Book of Daniel* was a Bible movie that took the viewer on the journey of Daniel's life as he served four different kings, spanning from Israel being taken captive to Babylon, to their release from bondage with the order to rebuild Jerusalem. This work of Christian cinema skillfully weaves the Scriptures together to tell one of God's most amazing stories.)

2006, Feb 19th, The Record

From: *The Record*, February 15:

Argument: See answering letter.

From: *The Record*, February 19:

The reply:

The letter writer of "Overdosed on Cindy Sheehan" needs to feel a little more gently and think a little more clearly about Cindy Sheehan.

Although she has lost her son, the letter writer sneers at her "pathetic puppy dog expression." President Bush started the unnecessary war and condoned Sec. of Defense Donald Rumsfeld's inadequate preparations for that war in which her son and so many others were killed. But the writer implies that it is not "President Bush's fault that [Sheehan son] was unfortunately killed in combat."

We need a better response to the terrible suffering this war continues to produce than can be supplied by a hard heart and a soft intellect.

Richard Lettis

Richard Lettis, Ph.D

2006, May 10th, The Record

From: *The Record*, (Your Views, May 7):

Argument: See answering letter.

From: *The Record*, May 10:

The reply:

The letter writer of "Clinton is no one to set moral example," called Bill Clinton "morally bankrupt," apparently because of his liaison with Monica Lewinsky.

If a sexual indiscretion can be thought to wipe out an individual's entire moral assets, I wonder what the writer must think of the account of the incumbent, George Bush.

President Bush has involved us in an unnecessary war, with thousands of deaths and injuries. He has led a campaign against scientists by refusing to join the effort to stop global warming. And — well the list hardly seems to end.

Now, there's a moral bank that has not only gone broke but has amassed a debt that may never be fully repaid.

Richard Lettis

2006, July 24th, The Record

From: *The Record*, July 17:

Bush has boosted U. S. Economy

Argument: See answering letter.

From: *The Record*, July 24:

The reply:

"Bring honesty to political debate"

"Bush has boosted U.S. Economy" (Your Views, July 17) attempted to defend President Bush against the charges of hurting the economy and failing to help in the Katrina disaster.

The economy has grown under Bush's leadership, the letter writer says, and it has been the Democratic mayor of New Orleans, not the president, who has failed "to take action."

I hope the letter writer has read "Budget fantasy" (Other editorials, July 18), which said that "Washington faces the weakest physical outlook in at least 20 years, and . . . the president has offered no plan to fix it."

He might also wish to read Douglas Brinkley's "The Great Deluge," which does hold New Orleans Mayor Ray Nagin responsible for much that went wrong, but also argues that the White House was, as one reviewer noted, "remote and unresponsive, viewing natural disaster relief as a distraction from the war on terror."

Speaking of administration critics, the letter writer urges, oddly, that there would be "a little more honesty on the left."

With all due respect, I suggest rather more informed argument on the right.

Richard Lettis

From *The Record*, August 17:

Argument: See answering letter.

Richard Lettis, Ph.D

2006, August 22nd, The Record

From: *The Record*, August 22:

The reply:

In "Evangelicals push for voters" John Paulton of Focus on the Family Action said he fears "what could happen if many more liberal politicians take over," by which he presumably means get elected by the people.

I wonder what he fears the fearsome liberals would do. Legalize gay marriage, which will no doubt harm his own marital relationship, although no one has yet shown how? Restore a firmer separation of church and state (which our wise forefathers established), thus damaging in some unstated way the church of his choice? End the legal imprisonment of accused and untried suspects, who languished in jail for so long some of them have committed suicide?

Darn those liberals. They sure are troublemakers, although they have not started and bungled a useless war, causing the world to hate us or — well, darn them anyway, let's not let them "take over."

Richard Lettis

2006, December 3rd, New York Times

From: *The New York Times*, November 19:

The argument:

Marriage has always been between man and woman, and must remain so. Gay marriage would be harmful for heterosexual marriage.

From: *The New York Times*, December 3:

The reply:

The Meaning of Marriage

The writer of a Nov. 19 letter would deny gays the right to marriage because ''you cannot change the definition of marriage.''

Of course this is wrong -- language lives not only by adding new words but also by altering the meaning of old ones -- but in this case our country and a good part of the world are trying not to change but to expand the meaning of ''marriage,'' so that any two people who love each other may gain the acknowledgment and acceptance of their union by us all.

I fear that the letter writer thinks this would be a bad thing. But if so he needs to offer a better reason than the definition of a word.

Richard Lettis

(There is some irony in the opposition to gay marriage for, at a time when marriage itself is considered by increasing numbers (especially of young people) to be unnecessary, the addition of gay marriages helps to support it. Perhaps also we may draw some comfort in finding that the anti-gays seem to realize that the condemnation of gay sex itself is close to disappearing, and so have turned to marriage as their best and perhaps last hope; we will see, below, an argument that children suffer from having gay parents, and that this claim has been strongly refuted. Fortunately this debate is now concluded: in isolated spots some who cannot bear change continue, but there have always been such--"the colored have always been inferior, "the woman's place has always been in the kitchen--" while society continues to acquire new understanding and helps life move on.)

2006, December 3rd, The Record

From: *The Record,* November *19:*

The argument:

Senator Cardinale urged the New Jersey government to put a "one man, one woman rule" in the Constitution, because that is what marriage has always been.

From: *The Record,* December 3

The reply:

State Sen .Gerald Cardinale, R-Ceskill, is right in urging full debate concerning gay marriage ("Put one man, one woman rule in Constitution" Other Views, Dec. 7)). But so far he has brought very little to the table for discussion.

His only argument seems to be that "the union of a man and a woman through marriage is a social institution that dates back through thousands of years," and so "should not be altered." By that same reasoning, we whites would still keep African-Americans in bondage, we Christians would still keep Jews out of our society, and we men would deny women the right to vote.

If history shows us anything, it is that to live well and decently, we must embrace change, at least in all areas in which some of us would have better lives, and none of us would suffer. No single voice has yet been raised with a real reason why gay marriage would hurt anybody, and it would undoubtedly improve the lives of many of our fellow citizens.

Richard Lettis

Richard Lettis, Ph.D

2007, January 31st, The Record

From: *The Record*, January 31:
This letter was not in response to another.
Comment:

A few recent letters in Your Views have used the term *Bush bashing*, implying that people are attacking the former president without cause.

In view of the Iraq debacle, the failure with Katrina, the abrogation of civil rights, the use of torture, the refusal to take global warming seriously and perhaps a dozen other matters, this seems puzzling. What would these writers require in order for President Bush to be rightly criticized? Perhaps if he engaged in illicit sex and then lied about it, for which so many Republicans became Clinton calumniators.

Richard Lettis

2007, December 18th, The Record

From: *The Record,* December 13:

The argument:

The letter writer criticizes the efforts of many people to deprive Christmas of its Christian spirit and make it just another holiday.

From: *The Record,* December 18:

The reply:

I understand how the letter writer and other Christians feel, because so much of our society turns Christmas "into just another holiday." But with all respect for her concern, I submit she must understand that many of us — Jews, atheists, Muslims, agnostics, secularists, Hindus and others — do not share her beliefs, yet feel we have a right to lay some claim to the day.

A celebration at this time of the year was begun long before the birth of Jesus, and while we have no objection to Christians who wish to call it theirs, and would do nothing to interfere with their ways of observing it, we must ask them to allow others to celebrate it in our way. In the spirit of the time, let there be peace.

Richard Lettis

2007, March 22nd, The Record

From: *The Record*, March 16:

The argument:

"Misplaced righteous indignation must go." The writer (and several other letters) attacked *The Record* because it criticized Attorney General Alberto Gonzales for dismissing several U. S. attorney s without apparent cause. The letter points out that it is the right of the Attorney General to make such dismissals.

From: *The Record*, March 22:

The reply:

Recent attacks on *The Record* for criticizing Atty. Gen. Alberto Gonzales illustrate how misinformation and insufficient knowledge can lead to wrong conclusions.

Yes, the firing of U. S. attorneys is a prerogative of the Attorney General, and has been done many times, but on this occasion the clear motive was not to clean house or remove incompetence, but a political move: The attorneys who were cited had not demonstrated political loyalty to the Republican government, and so were being fired. This is not a crime, but it is a deplorable intrusion of politics into the justice system, and *The Record* was justified in condemning it ("no place for politics," Editorial, March 15).

From: *The Record*, August 12:

'Megachurch cancels services for homosexual veteran."

The argument:

The letter supports the High Point Church's reneging on its promise to bury a gay serviceman, saying that to do so would be contrary to its right to freedom of religion.

From *The Record,* August 16:

The reply:

I know that the word *outrageous* is overused, but that is the only word that the refusal of the High Point Church in Texas to make good its promise to hold a burial service for a Navy veteran is because he was a homosexual. The excuse of church officials: They can't "condone" his sexual lifestyle.

The fact that a man served his country is less important than his sexual orientation, which is intolerable. A burial service is not approval of. It is merely a consecration afforded to the dead.

I fear the God of the High Point Church has a very narrow margin for the salvation of souls. But perhaps a greater God will have an equally stern limitation for those who tell a grieving sister that her brother has been denied his last rites.

Richard Lettis

Richard Lettis, Ph.D

2008, April 6th, The Record

From: *The Record,* March 31:

The argument: See answering letter.

From: *The Record,* April 6:

The reply:

A Democratic voter recently wrote that he would not vote for Senator Barack Obama because of "his background." Such a viewpoint is less than helpful to those trying to make up their minds. Exactly what is it in Obama's background that makes him not only objectionable but unelectable?

Surely it is not his mixed race; we must all hope that in the 21st century we have left behind such things. So is it perhaps his refusal to totally repudiate the former Minister of his church because he spoke harshly of our country? Other letter writers have said they would have walked out on a man who said such unfortunate things+. But they forget that this Reverend brought Obama into the Christian faith, led him to a spiritual life and became a close friend, and that the senator also refused to distance himself from a white grandmother who often made racist remarks.

Give one pause about voting for such a man? Possibly. But prefer to vote for another who would continue to sacrifice Americans in Iraq and keep the same lower taxes that favor the rich and hurt the rest of us? No one should think of such a thing.

Nor should those other Democrats who, like children refusing to play if they can't have their own toys, say they will not vote for another Democratic candidate in the primary if theirs loses. The difference between the two parties is far too huge and important for such small-mindedness. + (The minister, speaking of the mistreatment of blacks, said that they had a right to "damn America.")

Richard Lettis

2008, June 11th, The Record

From: *The Record*, June:

The argument: See answering letter.

From: *The Record, June* 11:

The reply:

President Bush, Senator John McCain and others who believe that
any dialogue between this country and objectionable governments (such
as those conducted with bad guys in the past by Presidents John F.
Kennedy, Richard Nixon and Ronald Reagan) is dangerous appeasement
should see a movie called "Babe," which came out in 1995.

The story concerns the need of the Master to get his sheep
properly herded. Two quite different animals were tried to this end.
One, two dogs, with considerable waste of time and effort, barked,
nipped and shocked the sheep into submission; the other, a pig, spoke
courteously to them and served the Master's wishes far more
effectively (and humanely).

In short, the movie suggested a choice between force and
persuasion, and opted for the latter. Now, granted, those whom Bush
and McCain accused of being or harboring terrorists are far from being
sheep. Still, it seems that talking to them, at least before we think
about loosing the dogs of war upon them, might be a good idea,
especially since we tried barking and nipping and shocking, and it
hasn't worked noticeably.

It seems a long time since I heard that adage about what a soft
answer can do with wrath. Perhaps we should bring it back into
fashion.

Richard Lettis

2008, July 28th, The Record

From: The Record, July12:

The argument:

("There is only one national anthem.") The writer criticized a columnist for arguing that René Marie had the right to sing the "black national anthem."

From: The Record, July 28:

The reply:

The criticism of Columnist Lawrence Aaron for defending René Marie's singing of the "black national anthem" failed to take American history into account.

In its celebration of "the land of the free and the home of the brave," the national anthem was a song for white people only. Blacks, the descendants of slaves, were second-class citizens, largely unable to vote, join unions, buy houses in all-white areas and, in more than a few cases, walk the streets of America safely+.

Who can blame people thus treated for thinking of a national anthem of their own? Though our country has taken great steps to end these conditions, by no means has racial equality become a fact for all today (how many black families are in your neighborhood?).

Surely the least we can do for a people as brutally mistreated as our African-American citizens is to allow a black woman to substitute the words she finds fitting for the national anthem.

+It is overwhelmingly disappointing to know, as anyone who reads a paper or watches TV news does, that black people still cannot walk the streets in safety, and still more disheartening to realize that it is some bigoted police who cause this.

Richard Lettis

Richard Lettis, Ph.D

2008, November 10th, The Record

From: *The Record*, November:

The argument:

The letter criticized *The Record* because it printed racist comments by some people just before Election Day.

From: *The Record,* November 10:

The reply:

I am sorry to see the angry criticism launched at *The Record* for printing the racist comments of a few people before Election Day. Of course, I understand how these writers feel, for almost all of us now are pained to see racial bigotry expressed.

But I want to point out that Mark Twain received much the same criticism when he incorporated the N-word in his "Huckleberry Finn." But he believed that his characters should speak their prejudices, partly because that made them more real, and partly because he felt racism is best attacked where is out in the open.

I assume *The Record* feels the same way. When poison enters our system, we don't cover up the boil and pretend it doesn't exist, but try to lance it and get the poison out. We must not pretend that racism no longer exists; we must recognize its existence in order to combat it.

Richard Lettis

2008, November 28th, The Record

From: *The Record,* November 28:

Argument: See answering letter.

The reply:

From: *The Record,* December:

"Correct adjective for Catholic Church"

In the same issue in which a writer criticizes *The Record* for printing a letter that spoke of the "inflexibility" of the Roman Catholic Church ("Only lip service to evenhandedness," Your Views, Nov. 28), "Catholic bishops campaign against same-sex marriage" (Page L-7, Nov. 28) reported that Catholic bishops are assembling a mass attack on the right of gays to marry. If one adds to that the fact that Catholicism still denies women entry into the priesthood, still would ban contraception, still silences any of its scholars who deviate slightly from church pronouncement and is headed by a pope who opposes flexibility in any form (this list is far from complete), the word inflexible seems not inaccurate.

Although many other religions strive with courage and compassion to shape their faith so as to meet and deal with the realities of the 21st century, Roman Catholicism remains, yes, inflexible, seeking to freeze us in an all-too-imperfect past. Its hold upon our culture has already slipped by a noticeable margin; if it continues its present path, it will eventually cease to be.

Richard Lettis

Richard Lettis, Ph.D

2009, January 10th, The Record

From: *The Record,* January 5:

The argument:

The letter deals with the problem of religious freedom versus the right to same-sex marriage.

From: *The Record,* January 10:

The reply:

"Boardwalk that will" said: "We support legalizing same — sex marriage. But we also agreed that religious organizations have the right to adhere to their own faith teachings."

Are you sure? In the past, some faiths have refused admittance to African-Americans, or stuffed them into the gallery. Would you, then, have supported them?

I assume some churches still would deny the marriage right to a racially mixed couple. Would you say they should not be "forced" to do so? And is the right of gay couples to religious union in the faith of their choice any less offensive to our moral convictions now than those acts are?

Consider: If heterosexuals commit any act the church deems wrong —lying, stealing, and abusing a spouse — does it have the right to deny them the marriage ceremony? And if not, why is the special "sin" of homosexuality acceptable reason for denial?

Why is it that religions are considered exempt from the regulations and practices that limit all other organizations? It is time to say that faiths may not be allowed to exercise beliefs judged by society to be dead wrong. Such actions may damage the fabric of our society.

Richard Lettis

2009, March 22nd, The Record

From: *The Record,* March 12:

The argument: See answering letter.

From: *The Record,* March 22:

The reply:

Commenting on Michael Spencer's "The coming evangelical collapse," a letter writer says, "he just doesn't get it" because "our faith isn't based on numbers." Well, yes, in considerable measure I think it is.

If the number of those evangelicals who decide otherwise continues to decrease as Spencer says, religion — with all its works, good and bad — must shrink to minority status and exert far less influence on our society than it now does.

This is already happening in Europe, where church attendance is nearing the negligible and is of less and less importance. Our Puritan past has kept theism alive longer for us. But we are the last great nation in which religion remains influential, and now we too, show signs of its weakening.

Some will hold onto their faith. But for many more of us, a naturalistic view of the world, without divine intervention, will prevail. The letter writer needs to get that.

Richard Lettis

Richard Lettis, Ph.D

2009, March 25th, The Record

From: *The Record,* March 25:

Comment on article:

Conservative Charles Krauthammer's shows him still to be the top candidate for the title: Man Who Doesn't Get It.

He is right in his observation that the bonuses given to AIG officials are, in comparison to the bailout money for the company, miniscule. But he is wrong in his conclusion that therefore it doesn't matter.

What outrageous us is not us the total amount, but the comparison of these bonuses to the desperate need of many for a small amount to keep our homes while the AIG executives by one more; to keep our jobs so they are paid for doing for one; and to keep our health benefits while they hardly notice the medical expenses they incur.

It's not the amount, Mr. Krauthammer, it's the difference. Try for once to understand.

Richard Lettis

2009, April 5th, The Record

From: *The Record,* April 2:

The argument:

The letter approves of the Bishops and writers of letters to *The Record* who have urged Notre Dame to reject Pres. Obama as speaker, because he advocates abortion and supports stem cell research.

From: *The Record,* April 5:

The reply:

I am sorry to see evidence that once again the irrational idea that to accept a person is to accept all that he is or believes.

Some Roman Bishops and a few recent writers of letters to *The Record* urge Notre The game to reject the President of the United States because he advocates abortion in some cases and support stem cell research.

To think about this is to see that makes no sense. If we were to follow it in all matters, we could hardly talk to each other, for few of us agree on everything. Shall we forbid a Catholic to speak at a Protestant university because he has the "wrong beliefs"? Shall we refuse to listen to a foreign head of government because he does not accept everything in our Constitution? If you and your spouse have not agreed on every single issue in your marriage, are you now separated?

Pres. Obama is doing everything he can to bring us all together, while some conservatives continue to attempt to drive us apart. Choose their way, or his.

Richard Lettis

Richard Lettis, Ph.D

2009, June 21st, The Record

From: *The Record,* June 12:

The argument:

In "Is Obama going too far in accommodation?" Charles Krauthammer criticizes Pres. Obama for balancing criticism of other countries with acknowledgment of certain faults of his own country.

From: *The Record,* June 21:

The reply:

Despite a few letters accusing it of liberal bias, readers of *The Record* should give it credit for attempting to present all sides of the political spectrum, as some occasional printing of syndicated columnist Charles Krauthammer demonstrates. I find this of particular importance in that it provides us with continuing evidence of how the Internet and misguided Krauthammer's thinking can be.

His most recent effort, "is Obama going too far in accommodation?", Argues that Pres. Obama — who in Krauthammer's singular mind considers himself "messianic" — has harmed his country by balancing his criticisms of Iran, Lebanon and Egypt with recognition of wrongs committed by the United States. Krauthammer fails to understand why Obama has done this and misunderstands his point.

Obama does not say all these wrong-doings are of "equal weight" but simply that, in a politically wise attempt to try honey where former Pres. George Bush's vinegar failed, he has diplomatically given up the "we are perfect" stance of his predecessor and is attempting to address the Arab world as one well-intentioned group of people to another. By means, for example, does Obama intend to say that the Muslim violations of the rights of its women are the same as the past lack of civil rights for American women. Only a jaundiced eye could fail to see that.

Please do keep giving us the columns of Krauthammer: It may well turn many of thoughtful independent away from any approval of the extreme right.

2009, July 17th, The Record

From: *The Record,* July 14:

The argument:

The writer complains that newspapers have been criticizing Sarah Palin.

From: *The Record,* July 17:

The reply:

Human nature being what it is, we will always find those who criticize members of the political party they oppose and are offended by any criticism of their own political side; it is like the baseball game in which the crowd moves the opposing pitcher for trying to catch the runner off first base, but chooses its own picture for doing the same. Thus, the same people who quietly accepted charges against former President Clinton and his wife now claim that the press is relentlessly pursuing Sarah Palin most unjustly.

Certainly the Clintons gave us some cause for adverse judgments. But surely Palin — who claimed international expertise because one can see Russia from her state, could not name a single newspaper she read, advocated a bridge to nowhere, was unable to use cite a simple Supreme Support decision, and has quit in the middle of her term as governor — the list goes on — is a worthy object for some criticism.

Far from "bashing" Palin, the continued attention of the press is due to her endlessly furnishing with quirky news items; all she needs to do to end the attention is to step away from her political office and retire to private life. (Or, stop doing screwy things.)

By all means, let their continued to be criticism from both sides against both sides. But will be accepted when it is due, and held to strict truth when it is given.

Richard Lettis

2009, August 8th, The Record

From: *The Record,* August 1:

The argument:

The writer issues various charges against Pres. Obama and Democrats, as listed in the letter of reply.

From: The *Record,* August 8:

The reply:

The word "chutzpah" (meaning arrogance, nerve) comes to mind when one reads the assertion that, "In six short months the president and this primarily Democratic Congress has managed to bring our country to the brink of bankruptcy."

Where has the letter writer been? For eight years, George W. Bush, with his costly war and his deregulation and other disastrous policies, did just that. To blame it on Pres. Obama, who is now desperately trying to repair as much of the damage as possible, is misplacing the blame.

Nor is it true that the Democrats "have taken over our automobile and insurance industries . . ." To begin with, what automotive industry is left to take over, after the myopic policies of the major companies have driven so many people to purchase the better cars made by other companies in other lands?

What should we do? Nothing, and allow our companies to sink deeper into disaster, laying off still more workers?

And oh, with that some brave soul living indeed "take over" the insurance giants, which have made billions of dollars by denying compensation to as many of us, as we are ailing, as possible (to which a former CIGNA official is now attesting) and which are so powerful that they may defeat Obama's courageous effort to control them. They may then keep their stranglehold on this nation.

Let us lay blame where it is due and give credit when it is justly deserved. Bush is the villain here, and Obama more like the hero.

Richard Lettis

2009, September 27th, The Record

From: *The Record,* September 19:

Argument: See answering letter.

All opposition is not paranoid

The writer finds a "dizzying symmetry in Joseph Chuman's argument" that we have "A creature of the left, demonizing creatures of the right for demonizing a president viewed as a creature of the left." He agrees with Chuman that some percentage of President Obama's critics are, "Nativists" who see a president with an international past as "other" and illegitimate, but argues that most of "those now in opposition to the president's policies, both foreign and domestic, cannot be so easily marginalized," for many are Independents who had voted for him.

The writer also says that "'Faith in reason' does not require dissenters to lay prostrate before the majority party's rhetoric." He points to huge deficit spending, "debt incurred in measures previously used to count the distance between stars, a constrictive energy policy that will cost families $1,700 per year while crippling private sector job creation," and "representatives giving an uninformed "bum's rush" to a smorgasbord of disjointed health care bills." more accurately explains the heated response we have seen in town halls this summer. Resistance to health care reform is aided by fear of paying for mediocracy.

Voters on the left, "see only hooded Klansmen, swastikas, impending violence and 'vast right wing conspiracies' in the current dissent," and they considered the 2008 presidential election to be" a mandate to reinvent America's wheel," which is proving to be "a colossal miscalculation." Some of them are in denial, and project "their own dark and apocalyptic fantasies onto the opposition."

Richard Lettis, Ph.D

From: *The Record*, September 27:

The reply:

The only thing of value in "All opposition is not paranoid" is its argument that we need to disagree in order to consider all possibilities in any case. But his description of Joseph Chuman's "Nation relives a more troubling aspect of its past" (Other Views, Sept. 19) as "a creature of the left demonizing a creature of the right for demonizing a president viewed as a creature of the left" is in all points incorrect.

Chuman and President Obama could only be characterized as leftists by someone so far right that he considers Senators John McCain of Arizona and Orrin Hatch of Utah to be card-carrying Communists. Our president has repeatedly attempted to consult Republicans in all that he has proposed, only to be stonewalled, almost every time. His recent appointment of Judge Sonia Sotomayor, whom no disinterested observer could call a leftist, is further evidence that the president is trying to make his way on a path between both extremes, as does his 2014 State of the Union address, in which he spoke of ideology from both the left and right as potentially damaging to the passage of a sound health care bill.

The only "demonizing" going on at present is the far right's wild claims of a health care death panel, a propagandizing of children, claims of denial of benefits to all Republicans and the truly mad characterizations of Obama as socialist, communist, Hitler and Satan. It is time for us to rebuff the extremists of the right, and do our president justice.

Richard Lettis

(Further evidence of Obama's centrality may be found in the many parts of his books that approve of compromise, and in his repeated declaration that there are no blue and red states, but just American states. As for the death panel, Sarah Palin achieved apparent immortality when she invented it, derived from some worries expressed elsewhere about the increasing costs of keeping the aged alive. It is hard to believe that millions of voters actually accepted the idea that the elderly would be put to death. Her rant was a notable example of the conservative practice of taking an inoffensive bit of information and twisting it into a devastation for humanity--Michele Bachman was also an expert in this kind of thing. Sometimes, however, things turn right in time: Bachman has left politics, and Sarah Palin has at the time of this writing spoken so distractedly and incomprehensibly that a number of Republican voices have disowned her. Truth shall out.)

Richard Lettis, Ph.D

2009, September/October The Yale Alumni Magazine

From: *The Yale Alumni Magazine*, September/October:

The argument:

A letter in the previous issue (September/October)) complained that the July/August article expressing pride in the University's advocating of gays was "the ultimate in boredom, and asked "Why must gays feel compelled to broadcast their sexual preferences -- and celebrate 'gay pride' months?" If the "editors expect readers to share their obvious 'pride' that Yale has become known for its gay promotion," the writer said, he and his colleagues felt "quite the opposite -- more one of disgust." My letter follows.)

From: The *Yale Alumni Magazine*, November/December

The reply:

There is an obvious answer to your letter-writer's question: They do so, sir, for the same reason we have "black power," the NAACP, and similar organizations for other peoples subject to prejudice. Like Ellison's message in *The Invisible Man*, these groups realize that if they are to gain equality, they must first be recognized.

As for another letter-writer's "disgust and repulsion," the gentleman might look to himself to understand why he has these feelings. Heterosexual couples have been known to perform the same sexual acts as homosexuals; do they disgust him too?"

If I at times am not happy with the erotic acts of some couples, I do not think my personal feelings should be enacted into laws depriving them of their civil rights. It is time that we leave behind the bigotries that, in the end, cause damage to us all.

Richard Lettis

(The occasional unhappiness I confessed to six years ago was due, I believe, to the many preceding years in which everything around me (including the) condemned gays as deviants. it took some time to work my way out of that conviction; even now I find vestiges in unguarded moments. But in the present I am able, instead of allowing it to sneak out in a letter, to throttle it. I was a child trained up in the way I should go, and it takes time and effort to depart from it.)

Richard Lettis, Ph.D

2009, October 23rd, The Record

From: *The Record*, October 14:

The argument: See answering letter.

Faith does not need physical proof. Regarding "Mystery no longer?" (Page A-10, Oct. 6), which calls into question the authenticity of the Shroud of Turin.

While the writer respects the difficulty of an "organization of atheists and agnostics that funded the research into the shroud to accept this image of Jesus Christ on linen" he argues that "an individual's faith isn't sustained by man-made objects. It endures spiritually. Faith is in one's heart, or it isn't." He believes that he was pulled through a medical emergency both by the doctors and also by his faith, for the doctors had told him he "should have died after reviewing their first evaluation." He accepts the necessity of agreeing to disagree about faith, but says that believers should not be insulted with "arrogance and ignorance."

From: *The Record*, October 23, 2009:

The reply:

I appreciated the calm and courteous letter regarding religious faith ("Faith does not need physical proof," Your Views, Oct. 14). But I have several questions to ask the letter writer.

Is he sure the faith he says he has in his heart was not instilled there in his early years, when his parents and virtually all of society taught him that all good people have it? If he had been born in a part of the world in which no belief in a god existed, would his heart still feel as it does now?

And is he certain that it is "believers" who need to be protected from the "arrogance and *ignorance*" of those whose hearts have not held his faith? I know of no atheist who has said he would not vote for a

Christian for president, but a recent survey showed that a majority of Americans would rather elect an incompetent religious candidate for the presidency than for a highly capable atheist. And we should not forget incidents like the one in which a religious crowd shouted insults while a father buried his veteran son.

Richard Lettis

Richard Lettis, Ph.D

2009, November 24th, The Record

From: *The Record*, November 24:

Only lip service to evenhandedness

The argument:

Regarding "Church inflexibility on key social issues" (Your Views, Nov. 24):

The writer declares that "The Record continues to shoot itself in the foot over its so-called 'unbiased coverage.'" She offers an example: When a Closter reader wrote a letter to the editor in defense of the Catholic Church, the headline it was given was a "snide dig at the church by use of the word inflexibility to describe the church's position," for the word "conveys a strong negative sense." Why would the paper not provide a neutral or even a positive term, such as "unchanging," "constant, consistent," "continuing," "unvarying," "firm," "resolute," or "fixed? as descriptive words? Of course, those are real possibilities. "But it's easier to let management print yearly maundering about how fair the paper is to all viewpoints without actually being fair -- especially where the Catholic Church is involved."

2009, December 6th, The Record

From: *The Record*, December 6:

The reply:

In the same issue in which a writer criticizes The Record for printing a letter that spoke of the "inflexibility" of the Roman Catholic Church ("Only lip service to evenhandedness," Your Views, Nov. 28), the article "Catholic bishops campaign against same-sex marriage" (Page L-7, Nov. 28) reported that Catholic bishops are assembling a mass attack on the right of gays to marry.

If one adds to that the fact that Catholicism still denies women entry into the priesthood, still would ban contraception, still silences any of its scholars who deviate slightly from church pronouncement, and is headed by a pope who opposes flexibility in any form (this list is far from complete), the word inflexible seems not inaccurate.

Although many other religions strive with courage and compassion to shape their faith so as to meet and deal with the realities of the 21st century, Roman Catholicism remains, yes, inflexible, seeking to freeze us in an all-too-imperfect past. Its hold upon our culture has already slipped by a noticeable margin; if it continues its present path, it will eventually cease to be.

Richard Lettis

(Needless to say, the present Pope strives admirably to decrease or end the Church's inflexibility, but he still faces an apostolic army of conservatives who try to defeat him. See my letter below for further comment on the problem Catholicism now faces.)

Richard Lettis, Ph.D

2010, January 8th, The New York Times

From: *The New York Times*, December 27

The argument: *Times* writer calls atheists "dyspeptic."

From: *The New York Times,* January 8

The reply:

Why is it that we almost never see the noun "atheist" without some pejorative adjective like "dyspeptic," which Judith Shulevitz shoehorns into her review of "The Faith Instinct" (Dec. 27)? Are the great majority of atheists really sour and sulky, angry and indignant?

Some unbelievers, uneasy at being the only group known by what it does not believe, have started the Brights, an organization that declares its faith in a natural world, without supernatural intervention; nothing sour there. The atheist Einstein professed awe and wonder at this earthly home of ours, and I have not read a word of grump in anything he -- or <u>William Butler Yeats</u>, or Matthew Arnold, or a clear majority of nonbelievers--has said.

C'mon, play fair.

Richard Lettis

2010, January16th, The Record

From: *The Record*, January 8:

Regarding Paul Aronsohn's "Cheney's comments on security muddle the debate" (Other Views, Jan. 5):

The argument:

The writer finds it "laughable that someone from the Clinton administration would actually have the nerve to criticize the Bush administration's handling of security threats and global terrorism, a term we can no longer use according to the Obama administration. He points to the fact that it was "the Clinton administration that was in charge during the '90s when there were numerous terrorist attacks, and adds that "It's a shame that more effort was put into covering up Clinton's affair with an intern than fighting terrorism." And there is no mention of President Clinton's failings. Former President Bush and Vice President Cheney, by contrast, "kept us safe after Sept. 11, 2001." He prays that the Obama administration "will wake up and realize that going back to pre-9/11 mentality is dangerous and irresponsible." It is Cheney who "has the guts to speak out and confront the naive view of our current leader."

From: *The Record*, January 16:

The reply:

"Say what you will about President Bush and Vice President Cheney," a recent letter declared, "they kept us safe after, 2001." ("Cheney doing what needs to be done." Jan. 8)

One is tempted to say a great deal. But surely the key word in the statement is "after." And yes, as the letter also says, there were terrorist attacks during Clinton's administration. But most of them were in foreign countries, where it is far more difficult to counter terrorism than in the homeland. In this country, just one attack occurred and with far less damage than the Sept. 11, 2001, horror, from which the Bush administration disastrously failed to keep us safe.

What Cheney is also saying is that we should return to the brutality of the past, that is, to torture, which a decent America had rejected by law years before him. In violating that law, Bush and Cheney became criminals, and those who continue to support them aid and abet breakers of the law.

The writer found criticism of these malefactors "laughable." Nothing to laugh about at all.

Richard Lettis

(When asked what he would do to punish the criminals, President Obama said he would take action if evidence was found, but wanted for the present to concentrate on contemporary problems. Lord knows he has had more than enough on his plate and perhaps was right in using his time to help the myriads of those who have suffered. Yet one may find it painful to recognize that if the offender is high enough, he may well escape the law. Also, we recall that President Clinton was close to impeachment for the rather less offense of lying about his sex life, leaving one to wonder what makes this difference between what Republicans can do without punishment while Democrats are relentlessly pursued (at a cost of millions). I think Clinton should have been formally reprimanded for his act--yes, the President shouldn't be allowed to lie--but trying to cover up a blow job is a long way from drowning possibly innocent men--not once, on some occasions, but more than a hundred times. By far the worst part of what Bush and Cheney did was to strike at the heart of the United States, depriving it of certain qualities that marked its greatness. No longer can we say all accused are innocent until proven guilty; no more can we declare that every person charged with crime will get a fair trial. We cannot consider our country superior to those which descend to torture. In the dubious name of safety, they have violated the principles by which our forefathers made us great.)

2010, February 12th, The Record

From: *The Record,* February 12:

The argument:

Regarding "White House moving trial of 9/11 suspect" (Page A-6, Jan. 30):

The writers finds "some truth in the argument that having the trial in New York City will focus the eyes of the terrorists (and the whole world) on the Big Apple." But this does not necessarily mean that changing the venue to Anytown, Miss., would make New York City a safer place. Sept. 11, 2001, for example was not "the outcome of a terrorist trial in New York City."

"We must be careful," he writes, "that while we engage in partisan politics, demagoguery and attempting to prove every decision is an incorrect one, we do not display a lack of resolve or willingness to combat and engage those who seek to destroy us." Though there is a reward of $25 million for the capture of Osama bin Laden, he is still at large. . . "In a fight against those who are willing to die for their cause, a 'vigorous' debate and petty partisanship may be luxuries we cannot afford."

We must suffer as we watch many venues offer a multitude of reasons why their locations are "not the best or most suitable for these trials." He concludes that "we may score minor victories against each other, but our common foe may take it as a signal that some of us do not have the stomach for the fight."

From: *The Record,* February:

The reply:

I am troubled by some things in "No time for high-minded debate" (Your Views, Feb. 8).

The letter writer argues that the suspected terrorists "started" the wars in Iraq and Afghanistan. Well, no, President George W. Bush did, and although most people agree the Afghanistan war was necessary, there now appears little doubt that the Iraq war should never have begun.

The writer declares that those awaiting trial "declared war on the United States by doing what they did." But isn't that what the trials are supposed to determine, and haven't they yet to begin? I remember some aphorism of my youth, now apparently long-forgotten, about the accused being "innocent until proven guilty." Too bad that idea isn't still around.

The writer also says that the accused, in declaring war, are "soldiers in al-Qaida or the Taliban." This is a case of one more misuse of words: no "war" was "declared," and the accused have never been soldiers. One does not declare war by an act, however horrible; a country declares by saying, "The nation is at war." And soldiers wear uniforms, carry weapons, do not purposely attack civilians, and do not conceal their identities.

We must restore words like war and soldiers to their original, proper use. And we must wait until a jury has reached a verdict before we decide who is guilty and who is innocent.

Richard Lettis

Richard Lettis, Ph.D

2010. March 23rd, The Record

From: *The Record*, March 16, 2010:

Compulsion is not sound policy

The argument:

The letter says that to call forcing everybody to buy health insurance or get fined "reform," is wrong: "All it does is add customers to the big insurance companies. Of course, that's why they make those campaign donations."

From: *The Record,* March 23:

The reply:

If the letter writer who objected to "forcing everybody to get health insurance" because "all that it does is add customers to the big health insurance companies" had paused for a moment to think the matter through, he would have saved himself time and concern ("Compulsion is not sound policy," Your Views, March 16). Here's why:

When those without insurance now get sick, what do they do? Either they go untreated and die, or they go to hospital emergency rooms. The insurance companies are delighted that these people were not obliged to take out a policy; now, the companies don't have to pay a penny of their medical expenses.

Who does? We do -- the writer, I, and other readers -- because the hospital can't afford to act as a charity and so turns to our government to cover the costs. The government pays, with our money.

It gets worse: People without insurance get sick more often than the insured do because they do not go to doctors for preventive treatment. Thus, there are more of them who need expensive curative treatment. And this treatment in emergency rooms is a far more costly means of restoring health than that provided by private physicians.

Result: Our country pays far more than any other for health and gets poorer treatment for its money -- so much so that this expense constitutes a major portion of our increasing national debt. This probably pleases the Chinese government, which lends us funds, but should be a matter of some concern to us.

Richard Lettis

Richard Lettis, Ph.D

2010. April 18th, The Record

From: *The Record*, April 14:

What Tea Party stands for:

The argument:

In answer to the question "What does the Tea Party stand for?" the writer says that "As an active member of many Tea Party gatherings and having attended many Tea Party organizational meetings in New Jersey," his answer is:

* The voice of the people.

* Less government intrusion in our lives and smaller government.

* Constitutional government and adherence to the Constitution.

* Liberty, the right of an individual to act according to his or her own free will.

* The freedom to produce, trade and consume any goods and services acquired without the use of force, fraud or theft.

* Capitalism and free markets.

* Stop spending our children's futures into debt.

* Lower taxes; no new taxes.

* Equality of opportunity, not necessarily outcomes.

* An end to elitist politicians who exempt themselves from the people's burdens.

* Absolute transparency in legislating.

* Free speech and an end to political correctness.

* Right to bear arms.

* Strong national defense.

* Honoring our obligations to our veterans.

* Secure borders; enforcement of immigration laws.

* Energy independence.

* Assistance to those truly in need of assistance.

* Individual responsibility.

"We members of the Tea Party in New Jersey," the letter concludes, "don't need someone to tell us who we are, nor try to co-opt leadership of the group: leaders will emerge and withdraw, and new leaders will take their places."

From: *The Record*, April 18:

The reply:

"What Tea Party stands for" (Your Views, April 14) omitted a few items from the list:

* Ignorance. One has to search far and wide to find a Tea Party member who really understands some of the things he declares himself against, like socialism (does the letter writer wish to kill off Medicare and Medicaid?) and the health bill (would the writer take back the insurance given to some 30 million people, or allow those who refuse to buy insurance to leave the rest of us to pay their bills?).

* Racism. The writer declares that people of all color are members. But some TV commentators and journalists say this is largely untrue, and I have yet to see a single black face in any of the clips or newspaper pictures of the protests.

* Hate-mongering. Drawings of President Obama as Hitler, false statements of the kind Rush Limbaugh and Bill O'Reilly and Glenn Beck spout, speeches attempting to replace reason with high incitement of passion -- these defeat the very admirable goals that I am sure Tea Party members at their best desire.

The list does include several good points, but they are ideas all of us support --e.g. adherence to the Constitution, freedom, and honoring our obligations to our veterans.

There is indeed a great deal wrong with our beloved nation today. But the way to a better America is not through the paths of vehemence, uncontrolled anger, and uninformed rhetoric.

Richard Lettis

Richard Lettis, Ph.D

2010, July 23rd, The Record

From: *The Record*, July 5:

The argument:

Charade of war in Afghanistan

The writer found General Petraeus's promise that we would have an Afghan victory to be "insulting . . . to the American people." Only the week before, he points out, the CIA had said that the Afghan effort was "mixed," which suggested, he said, that there was "no way America can win the war. Either Gen. David Petraeus is purposely misleading the American people under the direction of President Obama, or the two of them have not been communicating right from the start. Either way, how much more can the American people take of this charade of a war? "As a candidate, he reminds us, "Obama was quick to criticize President Bush," but when he became president, he found "the perspective to be a bit different from the helm." At a time when the nation is facing its greatest test, "America desperately needs a leader."

From: *The Record*, July 23:

The reply:

When he campaigned for the presidency, Barack Obama was "quick to criticize" George W. Bush, a recent letter notes ("Charade of war in Afghanistan"). Well, yes -- along with a goodly number of newspaper editorials, magazine articles, and not a few TV political analysts. Among other things, many of these condemned Bush's virtual abandonment of the valid effort in Afghanistan in favor of a totally unnecessary war in Iraq.

Now, as President Obama tries to end the wars Bush started, he stands in Bush's shoes the letter says, mocking Obama for finding the task almost impossible. But Bush's shoes took Obama to Iraq, leaving an ever worsening situation in Afghanistan for him to deal with.

It seems not quite fair to sneer at a man for having difficulty cleaning up a mess his predecessor left him. But some desperate Republicans are hardly concerned with fairness as they seek any possible reason for attacking our president.

Richard Lettis

Richard Lettis, Ph.D

2010, August 24th The Record

From: *The Record*, August 13:

The argument:

In a curious letter the author criticizes a former one which urged the removal of an effigy of President Obama at which balls were thrown. He seems to argue that the game is justified by the fact that the Obamas took "Golf outings, vacations in Spain," and charged "the mainstream media" with having "a ban on lobbing criticism at the president or his wife no matter how deserved."

From: *The Record*, August 24:

The reply:

What single thing could President Obama do, I wonder, without precipitating a flood of letters replete with condemnation? The president has received more scathing criticism in less than a year than his predecessor was given in eight years.

The latest crime of Obama and his wife seems to be that they take vacations: one critic complains about their golf outings and time spent in Spain ("Media fire blanks on Obama," Your Views, Aug. 13). I don't recall conservatives expressing indignation when his predecessor nearly set a record for time away from the Oval Office.

The letter argues, incredibly, that the anger aroused by an Obama figure, set up as a target for a Boardwalk concession on the Jersey Shore, is but another item in the "ban on lobbing criticism" under which The Record and the rest of "the mainstream media" operate. Shall we heave rocks for a while at the image of Dubya to see if the writer approves?

All one can conclude is that this writer's reading of The Record has been occasional and selective, for it -- and all the media -- has printed frequent articles criticizing the President. The Record's providing space for this ranting letter is in itself a refutation of the writer's argument.

Richard Lettis

2010, October 29th, The Record

From: *The Record*, October 11:

The argument:

Democrats cause their own problems

The letter argues that the claim Democrats are making in the
media, namely, that "evil Republicans have been blocking the great
work they are trying to do," is spurious. He claims that they say that
Republicans afford them no cooperation, and they have "even dusted off
former President Jimmy Carter to come to President Obama's defense."
But the truth, the writer says, is that it is the Republicans who have
no power. He points out that "Democrats have had a majority in the
House and Senate since 2008," and legislation has been held up because
of disagreement within their own ranks. They will not admit this, and
the" mainstream media appear unwilling to cover it."

From: *The Record*, October 29:

The reply:

I object to the tone of "Democrats cause their own
problems" (Your Views, Oct. 11). In place of the calm voice and
reasonable argument we so much need now, the letter writer says the
Democrats speak of "evil Republicans," sneer at "the great work" the
Republicans are trying to accomplish, and have "even dusted off Jimmy
Carter to come to President Obama's defense."

If one can judge by most letters to The Record, evil is a word
far more often used by Republicans than by Democrats. And to speak of
"dusting off" President Carter is snide and unworthy of anyone
courteously attempting to make a political point in this trying time.
Self-righteousness is a luxury we really cannot afford.

Richard Lettis

Letters to the Editor

2011, January 18th, The Record

From: *The Record*, January:

The argument:

Silencing by conciliation?

The writer tells us that on December 16, "some 2,300 veterans and families marched in heavy snow through Lafayette Park to the White House. We protested the wars in Iraq and Afghanistan. These are the most wasteful conflicts in our history." More than 4,000 Americans, he points out, are dead, and many others have suffered mutilation, while an accurate count of dead and injured Iraqi and Afghani citizens has yet to be counted. More than 100 marchers protesting the war were arrested for the "crime" of grasping the White House fence; the writer was "one of the 31 who chose to be charged and return for a court date. We wanted a venue to speak to the constrictions of citizen speech, lawful movement and right to assemble. These are the very bases for the American Revolution." True, the charges were dismissed on a processing technicality, "but was this response in fact another piece in our government's goal to totally silence opposition?" Perhaps this citizen action (one of many) "warrant overview by the Fourth Estate. A voiceless citizenry is a citizenry in chains."

From: *The Record*, January:

The reply (This letter is unavailable; I will try to recreate it from memory):

It would be painful to argue with someone who has so committed himself to his cause; one would rather write a letter of praise. But I do differ with the writer concerning his suspicion that the arrest of those who clung to the Whitehouse fence is a form of governmental act to foil the voice of opposition. Obama's life has been threatened, and anything that possibly resembles attack upon the Whitehouse is

95

understandable. And, the newspapers and political TV shows carry enough in one night to refute this claim. Indeed, perhaps President Obama has been criticized more than any preceding president. And there have been several group protests concerning the war. But do I favor this protest? I tend to do so, but wish the government would make its case for us, so we could better respond. I would, instead of complaining about censorship, criticize Obama's regime for failing to speak fully and clearly to us when an issue is debated.

From: *The Record*, January 10:

The argument:

First expression of 'don't ask' repeal.

The writer calls it a "disgrace" for the Navy to "fire a distinguished officer over a video deriding homosexuality that was made five years ago and was intended to raise morale among the crew." ("Navy captain fired for offensive videos," Page A-9, Jan. 5). He defends the video, which was strongly anti-gay, first by saying the "average crewman" (by which he would seem to mean heterosexual) would simply find it funny, and then by arguing that "If a small minority objected, it should learn to live with it," because gays constitute "only 2 percent of the population," and "it is ridiculous that their views should prevail over those of the majority." This, he concludes, "is possibly the first publicized ill effect of the repeal of 'don't ask, don't tell.'"

From: *The Record*, January 18:

The reply:

I am in some agreement with the letter that protested the firing of a naval officer who showed a video of questionable taste on his ship ("First expression of 'don't ask' repeal," Your Views, Jan. 10): We are all too sensitive about anything that has a sexual reference.

But when the letter writer refers to the part of the film that is homophobic, he and I part company.

He says: "If a small minority objected it should learn to live with it. With homosexuals constituting only 2 percent of the population, it is ridiculous that their views should prevail over those of the majority."

The estimation of the number of homosexuals actually ranges from the writer's 2 percent to 13, with almost all experts confessing that it is very difficult to decide on a precise number. And it is also hard to know whether a "majority" of Americans do or do not accept homosexuality -- the last estimate I saw said more and more do not oppose it. We are not talking about mere "views" here, but of bigotry.

We no longer tell African-Americans or Puerto Ricans or abused women to just "live with it," a phrase as hard and unfeeling as can be wished away. Our nation's history is one of incessant attempts to widen the circle of those afforded their freedom and civil rights, and the tiniest percentage of the population has the right to representation. It is sad to see some biased people still trying to shrink the circle it has been so difficult to expand.

Richard Lettis

2011, January 20th, Suburban News

From: Ramsey *Suburban News*, January 20:

To the Editor:

I am disturbed to notice that whenever a political cartoon is pictured in the Suburban News, it is of a conservative bent. The January 6 Suburban News cartoon attempts to demonstrate that despite the overwhelming majority of scientists who argue differently, the recent cold weather and heavy snow are evidence that global warming does not exist.

The truth is that the increase in snow is evidence for, and not against, global warming. When ice melts at an excessive pace at the poles, much of the moisture rises into the air, where it turns into snow and falls upon us more heavily than usual.

I am all for the presentation of political cartoons, but it is the responsibility of a good newspaper to be impartial, to present opinions from both sides of the political spectrum. I hope that the Suburban News will begin to do this in the near future.

(It did stop the one-sided printing of cartoons, but only by having none at all. Preferable, but not what I had in mind.)

2011, Febuary 24th, The Record

From: *The Record*, February 17:

Obama should look first to America

The argument:

"What is wrong with our president?" the writer asks, declaring he is "sick of him being an American apologist or expounding on the virtues of some other countries." In particular, he is offended by Obama's saying that "Egyptians have inspired us, and they've done so by putting the lie to the idea that justice is best gained by violence."

This offends his belief that "Americans inspire others; we do not get inspired by others." He goes on to say that Americans already know that nonviolence can cause great change," but then declares that "it is naive for the president to infer that non-violence is the only proper way to bring about justice, and goes on to provide several examples of troubles which did indeed require violence. He concludes by suggesting "that Obama look at our own history and stop apologizing to the world."

From: *The Record*, February 24:

The reply:

Surely, President Obama in his two years in office has been subject to more criticism than any other president had in eight years of service. And much of this criticism has been of the most trivial and mean-spirited kind.

The latest critic says in "Obama should look first to America" (Your Views, Feb. 17), that he is "sick" of Obama's "expounding on the virtues of some other countries." Well, that's getting ill rather easily, for Obama has done so only a few times. Perhaps the critic prefers President Bush, who in his time in office managed to alienate virtually every other country in the world. Which is better for the homeowner, to growl at his neighbors or to get along with them?

The criticizer objects to Obama's comment that "Egyptians have inspired us," because "Americans inspire others; we do not get inspired by others." Surely this is the worst kind of chauvinism. It argues that, unlike the rest of humanity, Americans are virtually perfect and cannot profit from noticing and acknowledging the good qualities of other people.

How sad it is to see such piddling remarks in a time when our president faces perhaps more daunting challenges than any of his predecessors. If we are as good as the critic says we are, surely instead of denigrating our leader we should get behind him and help him make us still better, for like every country we do have need for improvement.

Richard Lettis

2011, March 27th, The Record

From: *The Record*, article, March:

The argument:

Mitch Albom, who writes for McClatchy-Tribune Information Services, sends us a heart touching article, which a brief summary cannot convey, on the subject of free speech. Writing of the incident in which the Phelps family, members of the Westboro Baptist Church of Topeka, Kansas, "whose leader, Fred Phelps, is a hatemonger of the lowest kind," picketed near the entrance to a cemetery in which Albert Snyder was burying his son, Matthew, a soldier, who died fighting in Iraq. The family screamed God hates fags!" and, held up "vile and disgusting signs," including one depicting two men having anal sex. Albom comments: "You can talk forever about the sanctity of the First Amendment. And then you talk to the father. You can patiently explain why even hateful protests must be protected. And then you talk to the father. You can boast of how America's freedom of speech inspires robust debate on sensitive topics. And then you talk to the father. And you're not so sure. Albom informs us that when Mr. Snyder brought suit against the Westboro Church, "The Supreme Court ruled in favor of Westboro in Snyder's suit against it this past week. Arguing the familiar point that no matter how ugly speech gets, it's still speech and we can't go limiting it, the justices voted, 8-1," the one dissenting arguing that the First Amendment "is not a license for the vicious verbal assault that occurred in this case." Snyder, he wrote, "wanted what is surely the right of any parent who experiences such an incalculable loss: to bury his son in peace." When Mr. Snyder went back to work, people said they didn't know his son was gay; Albert Snyder said. "He wasn't. But anybody riding past that scene, that's the first thing they're going to think." Albom asks, "Do the ideals of

robust debate and varying points of view really apply to pure,
unadulterated hate -- the kind Westboro spews, claiming our children
are raised for the devil and that God hates America?
Sure, there is sanctity to the First Amendment. But isn't there
sanctity to a funeral, to a family's right to grieve in peace?" He
mentions other facts--Mr. Snyder says some day someone will bring a
gun to a similar burial, and the Supreme Court is by its high position
insulated from similar treatment, and a parent told Mr. Snyder that
his son
came home from school and said, 'I guess we can bully anyone now,
because it's free speech." Albom concludes, "The easy thing in a
newspaper is to say you understand, nod your head sympathetically, but
support the sacred right of free speech, which, after all, is a
cornerstone of what we do. Some in our business even don a cape of
nobility when defending it. . . . You can talk all you want. Then you
listen to the father. And you know this is wrong."

    From: *The Record*, March 27:
    The reply:
    Free speech comes at a painful price, but we can improve our
society only if we are willing to pay the cost.
    What right does free speech give? The recent outrage at the
disturbances that the Westboro Baptist Church has caused at the
funerals of a gay veteran has turned our attention once again to the
question of exactly what free speech gives us the right to do. Are
there not some utterances so reprehensible that we should be permitted
to silence them? Why should anyone have the right to express pleasure
in the death of an American soldier?
    Syndicated columnist Mitch Albom has written a moving article in
which he says that no one has such a right ("Free speech for vile
bullies," Other Views, March 8). He speaks commendably of the dead
soldier's father, who was obliged to bury his son while a group of

people stood by with shouts and signs celebrating the death of the young man because he was gay. Of course we and Albom sympathize with the parent, but we must also ask where his desire to prevent such action leaves the issue of free speech.

Two things in Albom's article are somewhat troubling. First, he speaks of the "sanctity of the First Amendment," an unfortunate use of the so-called loaded word that in this case would to some degree prejudice the reader against free speech. No one I know of has suggested that it is sacred, only that it is, in some form, essential to the exercise of a free nation.

Albom goes on to express something of a sneer at those who "don a cape of nobility when defending" free speech. This tone is not in keeping with the earnest good will with which he expresses his sympathy for the father of the fallen soldier. And surely those who are called upon to support the freedom of expression have the right to feel some pride in what they do.

Second, Albom gives slight attention to the question of why we need free speech. The closest he comes to doing so is this: "The easy thing [in response to objectionable utterance] is to say you understand, nod your head sympathetically, but support the sacred right of free speech, which, after all, is a cornerstone of what we do." His article would have been much better had he attempted to assess what this cornerstone means to our country.

I suggest two vital things that free speech means for us. While it obliges us to give reluctant support to the right to make offensive statements, it does so in order that the individual who, from time to time, urges something that the rest of us fail to understand as true, but is important and needs to be expressed, may do so. We must endure the bigot's rant, the sexist's sneer, the homophobe's disparagement, so that the young woman who is today sharpening and deepening her understanding, may come to see and be free to criticize something in our society that is damaging to us but that we do not as yet find harmful. There are such things. We may find the woman's declaration offensive in some way, but we will suffer if we do not allow her to speak.

Yes, free speech comes at a painful price, but we can improve our society only if we are willing to pay the cost. What is at first seen as the worst that can be said, free speech in permitting it to be heard may show us that its effect is salutary, that it brings to our attention some deplorable elements and damaging faults of our society. And when it fails to do so, it should oblige us, if we are good citizens, not to censor but just to speak out against such objectionable material. A boil can only be treated when it is brought to our attention so we can have it lanced, letting out the poison; to remain silent leads to greater illness.

As to the matter of the Westboro kind of incident, we are after all not helpless: If we are good citizens, we can raise a national cry against the ugly things that have been said and, it is hoped, shame the perpetrators into silence (possibly even change their minds). If they possess some intelligence, we can reason with them. We can enfold the grieving parent in our collective arms and drown out the voices of the warped detractors with our sympathy. When we hear of the potential disturbance such as that at Westboro, we can be present at any future repetition and engage and distract the demonstrators, countering the scandalous shouts with our own voiced respect for the dead.

If this is not always feasible, we must nevertheless continue to guarantee the free speech of all. It is indeed a cornerstone, and without it our mighty nation would stand in danger of losing the freedom that, perhaps more than any other nation, it has worked so hard to extend to all.

Richard Lettis

2011, April 23rd, The Record

From: *The Record*, April 3:

The argument:

Impossible to pin down Obama.

"Could you imagine what the headlines would have read if George W. Bush were president when the United States led the air attack on Libya?" this letter asks. She says she is puzzled by the fact that everyone accepts what the President says, and adds that "when he does speak he doesn't say anything." He gives examples, and concludes by saying "I listen to his speeches hoping to understand what it is he stands for. And each time I have to ask, "What did he say?" Nothing -- he says nothing?"

From: *The Record*, April 23:

The reply:

"Impossible to pin down Obama" (Your Views, April 3) asks an astonishing question: "What is it about President Obama that people feel compelled to back off and accept whatever he says or does?"

To ask such a question is to admit that one has not read a newspaper or watched a TV news program for the last two years. Anyone who has done so would surely have heard of the congressman who disgraced his House by shouting, "You lie," when the president made a State of the Union address. Surely, the fact that the Republican Party has voted down nearly every proposal that Obama has tried to pass would have been noticed.

The prime reason for the existence of the so-called Tea Party has been to challenge and degrade virtually everything that the president has tried to do. It would take a very long letter to enumerate all of the instances of opposition to Obama in the short two years in which he has been in office.

Richard Lettis, Ph.D

That any literate individual could with any seriousness ask such a question raises doubts about the welfare of our country. We need to find a way to educate our citizens, of whatever party, to overcome the biases that cause some of them to speak and vote against a candidate from the opposite party without reason. We are in a perilous time, and only dispassionate, careful, objective thinking will bring us through.

Richard Lettis

(I was at a loss to comment on the letter's arguing that Obama never says anything. The only answer would have been to print a number of the President's speeches, pointing out the many things he does say, clearly enough except for one of the many who can give him no credit for anything, and limited space prevented that.)

2011, May 10th, The Record

From: *The Record*, May 5:

Answers led to more questions.

The argument:

"When Barack Obama was elected," the writer says, "I accepted him as our president" because his mother was American. But the fact that "so much noise has been made in defense of his birth" raised his doubt. He criticizes the media for calling the Tea Party members "birthers," and wonders why it took 2 1/2 years to come up with a . . . birth certificate." Donald Trump, he says, "is right in asking that the validity of the document be verified."

From: *The Record*, May 10:

The reply:

I take no pleasure in calling names, but the two recent letters about the birthplace of our president can only be described as expressing willful ignorance, for whatever reason, about Barack Obama ("Answers lead to more questions," Your Views, May 5).

The first takes comfort in the fact that Hillary Clinton, three years ago, also raised this question, ignoring the obvious reason — namely, her desperate reaching for anything to combat an increasingly successful opponent.

The letter also asks, "Why did Obama wait 2 1/2 years to answer the question about his birth certificate?" The better question would have been, "Why was it necessary for him to even answer such a question, when there was no shred of reason to ask it to begin with?"

The second letter is almost worse. It says that we should wonder about Obama's birthplace because "so much noise has been made in defense of his birth"--another question, which one is almost embarrassed to answer: "Far more noise has been made by unfounded doubts of his birth; nothing need have been said if citizens had accepted the first evidence offered that Obama was born in the United States." How the mere making of noise can lead to doubt is beyond me. History is full of screaming suspectors and unreasoning denouncers whose ridiculous charges have been eventually mocked into silence.

This incredible refusal to accept any of the evidence that has been raised since the question was first asked raises one more question: "Why?" No certain answer can be given, but the uncomfortable possibility is that at least many of the doubters have done so because they did not think a man of color could be president in their lifetimes. No doubt some of this is subconscious, the speaker sincerely convinced he or she is no bigot. But the ill effect remains the same. It is sad to think that we as a nation may not have gotten beyond that.

Richard Lettis

From: *The Record* June 23 (second letter):

"According to President Obama," the writer says, "ATM's have helped create unemployment because they have replaced bank tellers." He claims that Obama is saying "that the unemployment rate is so high during his administration because of a 35-year-old invention." He points out the "economic benefits these machines add to the economy -- they need to be built, installed and maintained." — Another benefit of the ATM is that "In the distant past people had to wait in long lines on weekends or during their lunch hours to cash a check or withdraw funds using a paper slip. So they would often put off going to a branch to get money. Now, they can get instant access to their cash."

2011, July 16th, The Record

From: *The Record*, June 28:

The reply:

The first letter in "For Obama, it's back to the future" (Your Views, June 23) says that "the time has come to stop blaming George W. Bush for all matter of economic ills." Really? We should forget that he involved us in two hugely expensive wars, at least one of which was totally unnecessary? We should put behind us the fact that his administration pushed for the reduction of government control over business, thus assisting in the disastrous economic events of the past three years?

In the second letter, regarding ATM's, one shakes one's head to encounter this statement: "As anyone knows, when you get cash, you spend it. Which of course helps the economy — something this president has obviously overlooked." It seems to suggest that the only way we can have money to spend is by taking it out of a machine, ignoring the functions of bank tellers, checks, credit cards, and the occasional paper bill.

Thus the assault upon our president goes on, turning a blind eye to fact and dispensing with common sense. It almost seems as though when Obama clears his throat, some basher will find a way to proclaim a fault.

Richard Lellis

From: *The Record*, July 12:

Finally facing grim reality.

The argument:

After some sneers at Obama's speeches, this letter argues that, contrary to the boasts of the President, "The economy is not as rosy as our silvered-tongued president has painted it." Obama must compliment his efforts because otherwise "how would he be able to push forward the rest of his agenda like health care, $17 billion in defense increases and climate change initiatives." But when "he has to make a deal with Congress to raise our debt limit he paints a different picture." What he proposed is like maxing out credit cards no end.

From: *The Record*, July 16:

The reply:

As two recent letters show, conservatives continue to attempt to convince us that all of the faults of the Bush administration should be laid at President Obama's door ("Finally, facing grim economic reality," Your Views, July 12), dumping upon us the effluvia of another desperate search for anything to criticize.

The first of these letters, which drips with sneers that do no credit to the writer, makes the same hackneyed claim that because the president is a good speaker, we may conclude that he has no other capabilities; even Obama's strengths are mutated into faults.

The second condemns Obama for "all the spending his administration did," not mentioning that when he took office our country was in danger of economic collapse and could be saved only by huge investments, which have succeeded.

"Wake up and smell reality," the first letter says. Ah, precisely.

Richard Lettis

2011, August 26th, The Record

From: *The Record*, August 4:

The argument:

Catholic group prefers Earth centrally located. (This article was not found, but the following news clip conveys its content.)

A small group of conservative Roman Catholics is pointing to a dozen biblical verses and the Church's original teaching as proof that the Earth is the center of the universe, the view that prompted *Galileo* Galilei's clash with the Church four centuries ago.

The relatively obscure movement has gained a following among a few Chicago-area Catholics who find comfort in knowing there are still staunch defenders of original Church doctrine.

Astrophysicists at Notre Dame didn't appreciate the group hitching its wagon to the prestige of America's flagship Catholic university and resurrecting a concept that's extinct for a reason.

"It's an idea whose time has come and gone," astrophysics professor *Peter Garnavich* said. "There are some people who want to move the world back to the 1950s when it seemed like a better time. These are people who want to move the world back to the 1250s. I don't really understand it at all."

From: *The Record*, August 26:

The reply:

One can see why Notre Dame astrophysicist Peter Garnavich cannot understand a small group of conservative Catholics who argue, here in the twenty-first century, that the universe revolves around the Earth ("Catholic group prefers Earth centrally located," Page A-15, Aug. 4). But upon reflection, the explanation becomes obvious.

Galileo's heliocentric system, countering religion's claim that the earth is at the center of everything by placing it in its actual obscure position, was a frightening blow to Christians, raising doubts about their God's rendering of humanity as all-important. Dumped on a small planet circling an ordinary-sized sun, it makes us poor animals seem rather insignificant, and the deity not quite so friendly. The Church could not abide such a challenge to its authority--for a second reason as well: until the seventeenth century, the Church was the unchallenged authority on every issue, and any evidence that it was wrong in anything could shake that power.

Christianity in general has always vigorously opposed any premise that diminishes the probability of a god, that reduces us all to feeble short-lived specks instead of blessed beings. The most important example of this today of course are the dogged denials of evolution, which has struck organized religion more forcefully perhaps than any previous scientific conclusion.

The overwhelming conviction by the great majority of scientists that Charles Darwin and Alfred Russell Wallace, the first proponents of evolution, are substantially right -- however debatable some points may be -- is still refuted by the godly. And although one can understand their desperation, they must also be criticized for, as Garnavich says, attempting "to move the world back into the 1250s."

Richard Lettis

2011, Septtember 25th, The Record

From: *The Record*, September 16:

(The following three letters all comment on the same incident in which a music minister felt obliged to quit his parish because the priest had spoken against gay marriage.)

Sermon spurs gay musician to leave Catholic parish.

The argument:

The letter criticizes Robert Russell, music minister of St. Joseph Parish for "rushing to hire a lawyer and issue a press release trumpeting his alleged victimization" by a sermon in which the priest condemned gay marriage. "All that Father Astarita did, the writer says, "was to faithfully proclaim the truth, preserved by the Roman Catholic Church and verified by human experience, that the institution of marriage is a sacred reality reserved for one man and one woman." The wrong was in the fact that the priest was "subject to harassment and criticism for merely proclaiming the truth.") The real issue, she says, is freedom of speech and religion, a concern which brave priests have faced in the past. "If we Catholics, and others of faith in God, do not speak out on behalf of Father Astarita, we will see those who wish to control push harder against men of conscience."

(second letter)

Telling truth on gay marriage

The argument:

A lady argues that "Robert Russell, music minister of St. Joseph Parish in East Rutherford, is probably well aware of the Catholic teaching on gay marriage," and suggests that "Russell should find himself a place in a church that condones gay marriage -- and don't let the door hit him on the way out." She supports the priest, Father Astarita, for "upholding the teachings of the Catholic church," and dismisses Russell with the advice, "if you don't want to follow the rules, leave."

The argument:

This letter argues that "Instead of rushing to hire a lawyer and issue a press release trumpeting his alleged victimization, Robert Russell, "should have prayed quietly about his response to the church teachings that were provided to him by his pastor, the Rev. Joseph Astarita." For "All that Father Astarita did was to faithfully proclaim the truth, preserved by the Roman Catholic Church and verified by human experience, that the institution of marriage is a sacred reality reserved for one man and one woman." He fears that we are "entering a dangerous period in history when a faithful Catholic priest is subject to harassment and criticism for merely proclaiming the truth."

From: *The Record*, September 25:

The reply:

It is sad to read the letters criticizing Robert Russell for expressing unease about the anti-gay statements made by the pastor of St. Joseph Parish ("Telling truth on gay marriage," Your Views, Sept. 18). All base their defense of the parish on the false conviction that religion is exempt from the kind of critical examination to which all other organizations and individuals are subject.

If the parish's statements had been racist, or anti-feminist, or — yes — anti-Catholic, would writers still say that Russell "should find himself a place in the church that condones" these prejudices, or that he should have "prayed quietly about his response to the church teachings," or that support of homosexuals is merely "politically correct," or that the church is attempting to "protect young students and parishioners" from some imagined evil?

One of the finest strands of human history is that which has opened society to more and more people whom it once, without

foundation, excluded. Those who oppose this commendable effort delay
our fine attempts to make this world a better place.

Richard Lettis

(I felt that I was doing a useful service in meeting and refuting
such letters as the one I answer above. But it has been somewhat
disheartening to see arguments repeated again and again, as is evident
in the continuing debate on gays seen in this collection. In one
letter I mock a writer for, like Sisyphus, who eternally tried to roll
a stone uphill, only to have it fall back, failing to make his
argument accepted. But this representation comes back to haunt me, for
I realize at last that I may push a topic as far as I can, then in a
few weeks see another letter repeating the point I had put down. I
take consolation only in the words of Don Quixote, who, in his
commitment "to fight the unconquerable foe," found reward. (The
quotation is not from Cervantes but the musical)).

2011, October 7th, The Record

From: *The Record*, October 7:

(The following letter was written by a guest, my wife, Lucy Lettis.)

At long last, the September 11 victim compensation fund reopened on October for claims from first responders who have developed one of the illnesses such as lung disease and chronic sinusitis, common among workers and residents exposed to Ground Zero. Federal officials say there is insufficient evidence linking cancer to Ground Zero — tragic for stricken responders/residents and their families who feel certain of the connection but cannot "prove" it.

Claimants must provide evidence of the time they spent at the site. The required length of exposure has been extended, and more illnesses may be added to the program in 2012.

One can't help but wonder how many eligible responders may have died between the closure of the original compensation fund, which operated for two years, and October 3. Other responders, along with workers who cleaned dust from surrounding buildings, were diagnosed during the interim and fear they may not live long enough to see the funds come through.

Having lost acquaintances and a sometimes lunch companion in the towers, I am as much a proponent of the Ground Zero memorial as anyone else. Completion of the memorial has seemed slowing in coming. But would it not have been better to slow it even further if doing so would have freed funds for attending to the needs of survivors made grievously ill because of the months they spent toiling in the dust? Is this the tribute 9/11 victims would have chosen?

2011, October 26th, The Record

From: *The Record*, October 26:

Less tolerance than meets the eye

The argument:

The letter writer of "An un-Christian intolerance" (Your Views, Oct. 18) disagreed with teacher Viki Knox's view that homosexuality is a transgression against God and his holy rules.

The writer said it "seems to me that Jesus was much more liberal than Viki Knox." The key word in that phrase is seems. Jesus doesn't display any ambiguity in the Gospels but is continually reaching out to sinners with healing love and forgiveness. But Jesus also is the person who clearly speaks about the need for his forgiveness of our sins. The result of not believing in Jesus' own words is the destination of hell, or more precisely, the unquenchable fire.

God is indeed intolerant of evil. It is important to know that God is as much about justice as he is about love. He brings together a righteous judgment and forgiveness through the risen Savior.

From: *The Record*, November:

Less tolerance than meets the eye.

The reply:

It is discouraging to find, this far into the 21st century, that there are those who still take comfort in the belief that when sinners die, they are condemned to suffer "unquenchable fire" ("Less tolerance than meets the eye," Your Views, Oct. 26). What kind of wickedness deserves such heart-sickening punishment?

For some, the answer is homosexuality, apparently a sin so reprehensible that it deserves eternal agony. But what evil is it to be gay? I have read and heard a number of assertions ("it is unnatural" and "gay marriage would damage heterosexual unions" or "children need a mother and a father," among them) but have never seen sound evidence of any wrongdoing by gay couples.

The homophobe always falls back upon the Bible, but there is no condemnation of homosexuality in the Gospels. And if we are to accept the relevant passage in the Old Testament, we would also have to obey such other commands as how to take care of our slaves, consider our wives as property, and slaughter all non-believers.

When one looks at well-known homosexuals in history, no more wickedness is to be seen than in heterosexual humans, and not infrequently considerably more genius, productivity, and humane behavior. It is time to give up this damaging bigotry, and accept one more group into respectable society.

Richard Lettis

2011, December 19th, The Record

From: *The Record*, December 11:

(This letter was occasioned by a proposed state bill that would establish certain conditions for capital punishment. The writer understandably argued that Morgan's crime, which was to "allegedly throw his child in a car seat weighted down with a tire jack into a brook to drown," was such that "giving him life in prison is not enough." He did agree with one point in the bill, namely, that "no victim should hold a greater weight"--that is, execution should not be limited to the killer of certain persons, for example a policeman.)

On the death penalty bill

Regarding "It's not justice" (Editorial, Dec. 14):

The argument:

The Record picked a bad time to express its views concerning the death penalty bill sponsored by state Sens. Robert Singer and Anthony Bucco using Arthur Morgan III, according to this writer. He would be shocked to hear that anyone would not want Morgan to be executed; a prison sentence would not be enough. Morgan "allegedly threw his child in a car seat weighted down with a tire jack into a brook to drown." What purpose, he wonders, does such a person serve by continuing to live? He is trash, and should be discarded. The point in the article that America is a vigilante country and individuals should not get to decide how someone is punished is answered by the article itself: "Criminal courts follow established laws. Who do you think makes the laws we follow? Individuals voting on established and proposed laws. So let's vote on it." The writer does agree with the article's point that "no victim should hold a greater weight, as the Senators' proposed bill seems to hold." limiting the death penalty to certain crimes, such as killing a police officer or someone younger than 18.

Richard Lettis, Ph.D

From: *The Record*, December 19:

Regarding "On the death penalty bill," Dec 14, 2011:

The reply:

"If there is someone in this universe who does not want to see [Arthur] Morgan get executed I would be shocked." So writes a devotee of capital punishment. I am obliged to shock the writer, for here is someone, and here is why.

We cannot afford to execute people for financial and moral reasons, financial because it costs more to execute a criminal than to put him in jail for life, and moral because the only motive for doing so is revenge. People speak of "closure," but there is no such thing as closing the book on the grief we feel for the child Morgan allegedly murdered. And revenge is condemned by the Bible, as does a number of other writings on ethical behavior.

"What purpose does Morgan serve by continuing to breathe?" the writer asks. The better question is: "What purpose does killing him serve?" His death would not bring back the dead child or erase her suffering. And execution would terminate Morgan's pains, while a life in prison would mean a long time of retributive misery.

One of the things civilization attempts to do as it strives to improve our lives is to bring an end to killing. That our government should continue this practice is a lamentable deterrent to that effort.

Richard Lettis

(The criticized letter, in its describing the crime of the accused, serves a severe purpose: it is hard indeed to resist the impulse to do away with someone who has done such a terrible thing. The commendable denial of death for such an offender does indeed not come easy. True of many essential things.)

2012, January 19th, The Record

From: *The Record*, January 11:

Regarding "Cuomo boosts hopes for bill on gay marriage" (Page A-3, Jan. 9):

The argument:

Listing some of the problems needing attention by New Jersey--"unsustainable debt, out-of-control spending, an unbearable tax burden, crumbling cities and infrastructure, failed school systems, ethics reform," The writer chastises the Legislature for spending its time on gay marriage. "It's unbelievable, he says," that these non-minds in Trenton would even spend more than a few milliseconds on this issue before moving on to making progress on any or all of the ills that beset this state." It shows the need for "term limits or other strong measures that would force the Assembly and state Senate to deal with fundamental responsibilities to manage affairs of state government. "All of this, he concludes, "is a diversion away from a consideration of the Legislature's ability to govern." It was up to the electorate "to force the legislators to wake up and do what they are paid to do."

From: *The Record*, January 19:

The reply:

The letter writer (Jan. 11) chastises the Jersey Legislature for spending time on the bill for gay marriage, arguing that this is a "diversion away from a consideration of the Legislature's ability to govern." It does seem excessive to say that giving attention to one bill proves the inadequacy of any government agency, unless of course the bill is wildly unimportant or wrong, which seems to be the hidden message of the letter.

Richard Lettis, Ph.D

Is the bill on homosexual union a waste of time? I suggest that if the letter writer had a gay child, or good friend, or even a likable acquaintance (as more than a few homophobes have, to their consternation, found they had), he would not think so.

What is at stake here is a matter of civil rights for a considerable portion of our population, and one of the tenets of our nation is the protection of the rights of all of us. A prospective bill would provide gay men and women with one such right, which must be considered as an important part of "the ills that beset this state" mentioned by the letter writer.

The Pledge of Allegiance affirms "justice for all," not for just some.

Richard Lettis

2012, March 24th, The Record

From: *The Record*, March 19:

The argument:

Replying to an article criticizing Rush Limbaugh, the writer says that "Your comments concerning civility in the Senate have nothing at all to do with Rush Limbaugh, but you so do wish with all your little hearts that it does become a battle cry for desperate Democrats in the fall." Actually, Limbaugh was correct in accusing a woman who testified before a Senate group, urging that insurance be required to cover certain cost related to sex. "Why," he asks, "should a mandate order coverage for your sex habits?" Men and women must continue to be responsible for their sexual acts, for if they do not, "it will bring an eventual breakdown of our social order."

From: *The Record*, March 24:

The reply:

Despite the occasional complaints by arch-conservatives that The Record gives them no space, the fact is that the paper, to its credit, does present both sides of the political spectrum. In the printed letters we may be given a truth-producing debate about politics. But a recent letter, "Limbaugh was right on Fluke" (Your Views, March 19) does nothing to further useful discussion. To begin with, it simply ignores the unfounded and insulting remark that Limbaugh recently made.

By snarling at "all your little hearts," the writer introduces anger into the argument, jettisoning reason (for the former diminishes the function of the latter). The question raised -- "Why should a mandate order coverage for your sex habits?"--hardly requires an answer. It is not a "habit" that is at issue, but the prevention of unwanted pregnancies, which in this time of overpopulation is of great importance.

The letter charges that men and women "want no responsibility for sex." It is difficult to understand the relevance of this assertion: few of us *want* to be responsible for much of anything, but we recognize the necessity and in our sexual lives succeed and fail about as much as in any other onus. Equally puzzling is the final claim that coverage of contraception will lead to "an eventual breakdown of our social order." To my mind this smacks of that puritanical fear of sex that persists in our society.

A wise man said that when a problem arises, "Come, let us reason together." Surely, this is a better thing to do than yelling.

(The event may not be clear: a woman testified before a committee, urging that contraception be given more coverage. Mr. (if we must give him a title) Limbaugh mocked the lady, said she obviously liked sex too much, and considered the possibility that she was a prostitute--another prime example of how some conservatives twist a simple fact into gross misbehavior. This was one of the few times in which a general reproach was leveled at The Mouth (I must stop; I am damaging reason by introducing anger.)

2012, April 25th, The Record

From: *The Record*, April 20:

Good reason for NYPD 'spying'

The argument:

The Associated Press's "uncovering" of the New York Police Department spying on Muslims," the writer declares, "has contributed to a threat against the United States."

Though the media "appear to believe they are 'doing the right thing' by exposing police and federal agencies," we must understand that "The fight on terrorism starts in our own country" and we must do what the Muslim community is willing to do. And so "We should be able to use the same techniques without being exposed' by overzealous reporters."

From: *The Record*, April 25:

Regarding "Good reason for NYPD 'spying' " (Your Views, April 20):

The reply:

The letter writer believes that we should spy on one particular group of our citizens in the name of security. I disagree.

One of the things that makes our country great is its ongoing effort to recognize the rights of minorities — among them blacks, women, Jews and homosexuals. It is regrettable that someone should urge us, as we continue to improve the civil rights of these groups, to go backward in another case, depriving one minority of its rights because a few of its members have harmed us.

What price are we going to pay for security? Shall we discard our national achievements, have less courage than that of our ancestors -- as well as that of the young people in Iraq and Afghanistan -- who risked and continue to risk their lives in defense of our civil liberties? We cannot be the land of the free unless we remain the home of the brave.

Richard Lettis

2012, June 19th, The Record

From: *The Record*, June 14:

Children's rights and same-sex marriage:

The argument:

"The best argument against same-sex marriage," the letter avers, "is that every child comes from and has the undeniable right to his father and mother." Children's right to this is "a fundamental right that trumps all the others." Adults, then, "do not have the right to [make] laws that would institutionalize the denial of that right." And the "Legalization of same-sex marriage is one such law."

From: *The Re*cord, June 19:

Regarding "Children's rights and same-sex marriage" (Your Views, June 14):

The reply:

The letter writer believes that gay couples should not have children. His intent is to outlaw gay marriage, arguing that it denies children their right to have a mother and father.* It is hard to see how this makes sense.

In this imperfect world, a child too often finds that he has neither parent; this is why we have adoption. Our overpopulated homes for orphans are evidence that there are not enough heterosexual couples to adopt all, and surely it is better for a child to have two mothers or two fathers than have no parents at all.

As a recent movie, "The Kids Are All Right," convincingly shows, the children of gay parents do much better than those left in public institutions -- indeed, they seem to do quite as well as the children of mothers and fathers. To outlaw homosexual marriage for the sake of children makes no sense at all.

Richard Lettis

*The charge that children suffer both physically and morally having been dismissed (see Toni Meyer, below); the homophobe has turned to one last use of children to attack gays. I have seen no more of this claim, so perhaps it joins its predecessor on the road to extinction.

2012, July 14th, The Record

From: *The Record*, July 14:

Tired of gripes about health care law

The argument: (see replying letter)

From: *The Record*, July:

Regarding "Tired of gripes about health care" (Your Views, July 14):

The reply:

It takes a good deal of chutzpah for the letter writer to argue that liberals were inconsistent in criticizing the Supreme Court before its recent ruling about health care and approving of it when its decision was known. Liberals had every reason to believe the court's conservative majority would dismiss President Obama's law and every reason to be glad they were wrong and to approve of the Supreme Court in its decision. If the writer finds this to be "mind-boggling," one can only suggest that in this, the mind was easily boggled.

And surely it takes considerable gall for a Republican to criticize anyone for a change of mind, considering the avalanche of changes his party has made concerning a number of proposals that it has in the past supported (and in some cases even initiated) yet now opposes, for no apparent reason other than the president has attempted to act on them. Surely, the GOP has won the prize for the number of flip-flops.

When Barack Obama was elected president, a Republican said his party would do anything necessary to prevent his second election. And in this it has been consistent, ignoring the damage done to our country for the benefit of its own party. Compared with this, a modest change of opinion about the Supreme Court hardly seems worth the writing of a letter.

Richard Lettis, Ph.D

Richard Lettis

2012, August 19th, The Record

From: *The Record*, August 14:

The argument:

It is plain and simple, the writer says: "President Obama is the 'food-stamp president' and Mitt Romney will be the 'paycheck president.' Obama has almost destroyed our country and is trying to make us like Greece. We need Romney."

Romney's wealth pleases the writer; it shows that "He knows how to create jobs and make money, and would do the same for everyone as president, giving Americans "the opportunity to create their own success stories." Romney's presumptive running mate, Rep. Paul Ryan of Wisconsin, is proficient with finances, and as a good family man would know how to help fix this mess. We need to get out of debt, give our children a better future without food stamps. "We need real leaders, not people whose leadership record consists merely of organizing, handing out pamphlets and trying to divide this country." This time Obama will not be able to hide from the mess he has made, which began with Obamacare.

From: *The Record*, August 19:

Regarding "With choice clear, Romney is obvious" (Your Views, Aug. 14):

The reply:

The letter writer said President Obama is "trying to make us like Greece," seeming to suggest, as Tea Party members have often done, that Obama hates his country and wants to ruin it -- that is, he endured the hard and painful process of getting elected just so he could destroy what he now governs.

What act has he committed -- no one has suggested any -- that attempts to damage the nation?

We may differ with some of his work, but it is the egotistical mind that claims to know his motive. Why would he be "trying to divide this country" -- how would he profit from such an act? Has he not, again and again, declared that there are no red and blue states, just American states?

Surely conservatism should be reproved for the many wildly unfounded charges of this sort. If the president is to be criticized, let it be by sensible and well-documented fact, not by off-the-wall, baseless assertions.

You are right: "The too-large numbers of Americans who are either unemployed or underemployed are not looking for elevators for their cars." They are looking for real jobs.

Richard Lettis

2012, September 16th, The Record

From: *The Record*, Sept 9:

The Problem with Obama's Rhetoric

The argument:

In this article, John Kass sharply criticizes President Obama on
a number of issues. Seen as "some kind of messianic political god,
leaving the enraptured throngs unshaken in their faith that every word
from his mouth was pure gold," Obama's government has, he says, left
"the multitudes . . . out of work. Reality trumps rhetoric."
Granted, "he pulled our troops out of Iraq, ordered the killing of
Osama bin Laden and passed that massive expansion of federal power
called Obamacare," which is probably enough to get him reelected. "But
at bottom he remains a man of rhetoric. And Americans can't use
rhetoric to pay their bills," nor does it "feed the kids or put gas in
the car or take care of the college tuition." Voters still want
change, "but they want the kind that's heavy in their pockets, the
kind that jingles, not the lint that's there now." Obama asked, in
his first campaign, "Do you think that you are better off now than you
were four years ago or eight years ago? And if you don't think you're
better off, do you think you can afford another four years of the same
failed economic policies that we've had under George W. Bush?"
Considering Obama's record, this is a piece of rhetoric showing that
"It often bites the man who reads it." After commenting on a speech
Obama had recently given (he mocks Obama for using a teleprompter)
which said that in the coming vote the choice would be not only for
one of two candidates but would "be a choice between two different

paths for America. A choice between two fundamentally different
visions of the future." Kass denies this: "a choice between a big-
government Democrat and a big-government Republican is a choice
between two horns on the head of the same goat. His Democrats use tax
dollars to buy votes with social programs. The Republicans buy theirs
with defense contracts. He turns to charges against Obama: "Under
Obama's watch, the national debt has ballooned, passing into the
trillions and trillions, numbers inconceivable only a decade ago. And
China holds our paper." Despite these failures, Obama offered only
"more government, not less, while parading that savage icon of massive
federal spending and authority, Franklin Roosevelt. Obama's message
Thursday was that he's not in the White House to sing soothingly to
us, but rather, he's been put here to tell us hard truths, even as he
offered muffled code words like "shared responsibility" (more taxes)
and "persistent experimentation" (more government). After telling the
voter that he would tell only the truth, the president said it would
take more than a few years to solve challenges that have built up over
decades. It will need "common effort, shared responsibility, and the
kind of bold, persistent experimentation that Franklin Roosevelt
pursued during the only crisis worse than this one." But Kass cites
historians who have "concluded that Roosevelt's big-government moves
only made the Depression worse, and that only a world war got the
economy going. But Americans are so tired of war." He continues to
cite presidential mistakes, and argues that, after the Republican
surge in the past election, he could have "change[d] political course
like a Chicago version of Bill Clinton, but he remains, stubbornly, a
man of the left, and government is the hammer in his hand.

"Hope may remain, but with Obama, change seems impossible."

John Kass writes for the Chicago Tribune.

From: *The Record*, September 16:

Regarding John Kass's "The problem with Obama's
rhetoric" (Opinion, Page O-2, Sept. 9):

The reply:

Kass does a fine job of exhibiting some of the faults of today's Republican Party. To wit:

* He sneers at the Barack Obama of 2008, calling him "some kind of messianic political God, leaving the enraptured throngs unshaken in their faith that every word from his mouth was pure gold." Republicans follow the same line of ridiculous overstatement by attempting to diminish what in reality is a fine quality. Fault: Nothing about Obama can be good, not even his strengths.

* He reduces Obama's many achievements to a mere three, criticizing one, health care, as a "massive expansion of federal power." Fault: Republicans similarly misrepresent and diminish any good accomplishment of the opposition.

* He says that the president "remains a man of rhetoric," and "Americans can't use rhetoric to pay their bills." Fault: reduce a multi-talented man to as little as may be believed, and pretend that we suffer because he can do, has done, no more.

* Obama "read his speech well Thursday, the winged words on a Teleprompter." Fault: mean-spirited desperate stretching for something to criticize (Republican speakers do not read teleprompters?).

Until recently, the Republican Party has deserved to be called the Grand Old Party. It has given our country some excellent statesmen and furthered beneficial legislation. But now, its only goal is the defeat of Obama, using any means, however wrong and contemptible, to that end, no matter how much doing so damages our country. We can only hope that the fine men and women of the party will eventually gain control again and allow our two-party system to function productively.

Richard Lettis

Richard Lettis, Ph.D

2012, October 16th, The Record

From: *The Record*, October 11:

The argument:

"One month before the elections," the writer says, "President Obama wants us to believe that the unemployment rate fell to 7.8 percent in September." But150,000 new jobs are needed each month in order to keep pace with the growing population, and only 114,000 jobs were created in September. The unemployment rate, he notes, went down from 8.1 percent only to 7.8 percent. The president' makes no sense. Our "dismal" economy is evident in the fact that only 63.5 percent of the working-age population is either employed or actively looking for work; this is a 30-year low. "The real unemployed/underemployed rate is 14 percent." Under Obama's government, median household income has fallen from $55,000 to $50,000 a year, and the net worth of Americans households has "plummeted" 39 percent, while the poverty rate has risen from 14.3 percent in 2009 to 15 percent in 2011. 46.2 million Americans now live in poverty, which is the highest rate in 52 years. "Is this the scenario we want for our country?" the writer asks, must this be the "norm" for Americans? He would welcome the failed policies of the Bush administration, "when unemployment was 4.7 percent and household incomes increased every year."

From: *The Record*, October 16:

The reply (which is to the above letter and two others):

Regarding "Romney-Obama: The battle goes on" (Your Views, Oct. 11):

It is tiresome to read in three recent letters the same old allegations against President Obama, all of which have been refuted several times. Let us try once more.

The first letter cites figures to show that the recent drop in unemployment is false. The fact that the lower figure was reached in precisely the same way it has always been done is ignored.

The second letter poses several questions, all of which have been answered more than once. To wit:

* "Are you better off today than you were four years ago?" No, but I am no worse off, as I would have been had the Republicans continued to govern.

* "What is the price of gasoline?" It is high, but has been getting higher ever since the 18 cents per gallon of my youth. Our presidents have never controlled the price of gas.#

* "Do you feel safer today than you did four years ago?" Well, I feel safer than I did before President Obama eliminated Osama bin Laden and energetically pursued al-Qaida.

* "Who is coming in over our unprotected borders?" I'm not sure. But whoever they are, they are probably the same kind of people who have come in the past, and are the ancestors of us all. Our borders are no less protected than they ever have been.

* "Are our overseas diplomats safe?" Not as safe as they should be. But making them safe, especially in hostile countries, is immensely difficult.

* "Why are so many Americans on food stamps?" Because former President George W. Bush and company wrecked our economy and caused many, many hardworking people to lose their jobs.

The third letter, which accuses the president of being "an actor playing the part in a very low-rated movie," simply provides us with one more example of the groundless name-calling in which some Republicans indulge.

This kind of thing has to stop; such comments contribute only to the harsh division from which we now suffer. Obama is not perfect, and informed criticism of him is important. Only when we can come to respect each other and offer well-founded and polite critical comment will we ever become again the great country we once were.

Richard Lettis

(#At this writing, the price of gas has lowered considerably; I
have not heard one Republican congratulate the president for his
achievement.)

2012, November 18th, The Record

From: *The Record*, November 11:

Reactions to Obama reelection

The argument:

President Obama's reelection, the writer says, "makes me wonder what American citizens are thinking." He decides that it is owing to their inadequacy for which he gives examples: dependence on government support, inability to do their own thinking get their own health care, get a job, or even feed themselves. He recalls John F. Kennedy's statement: "My fellow Americans, ask not what your country can do for you; ask what you can do for your country," whereas now, people say "What can my country give me, and what can I get for free?" They have become zombies. "We are turning into Europe,' he declares, where "an Obama-style health care [is] bankrupting countries."*

From: *The Record*, November 18:

Regarding "Reactions to Obama reelection" (Your Views, Nov. 10) and "In wake of Election 2012" (Your Views, Nov. 11):

The reply:

Letter one argues that those who voted for President Obama "cannot think for themselves," by which, one assumes, he means that they cannot think as he does. These voters also "cannot get a job on their own, they cannot feed themselves." So, it would seem, all those who voted for Mitt Romney managed, despite the economic collapse, to get jobs and afford food? Nothing wrong here?

Another letter called Obama a "proven liar," though one would think, in consideration of the many lies Romney told during the debates, that a Republican might be embarrassed to raise the subject of falsehood.

Still another argues that "we will all pay dearly" for this

"misguided election." Prediction is an uncertain act. But my guess is that, at the worst, we will not pay as much as we did for the -- as even some Republicans now admit -- agonizingly misguided election of their last candidate.

Another said those who voted for Obama have "rejected God's help and direction." Is there not a certain amount of hutzpah in a political party that claims to know what God's political inclinations are? Considering the fact that the Republican Party supported the candidacy of a man who called rape "an act of God," it would almost seem that credence in a divinity would also be a subject that party would avoid. And in truth, the Democratic platform contained a number of references to faith.

Why all this vituperation? Doesn't it seem rather like the ranting of sore losers? A sharp contrast is provided by those Republicans who are now saying that their party needs to adjust itself to the greatly changing country that we now are. It sounds a great deal more promising -- and commendable -- than reasonless name-calling.

Richard Lettis

(Letters such as the last here are frightening. Some of our fellow-citizens, perhaps a large number, reveal a fuzziness, a confusion of perception, There is nothing whatsoever in Barack Obama's public or private life to suggest remotely that he rejects any part of the deity; he is a regular attender of a Christian church, and calls upon God's blessing for our country at the end of each speech. What help, specifically, is it that he is said to reject--what did God have in mind for us, and how did Obama refuse to execute it? What directions did God give specifically to the United States? These are obviously unanswerable questions, for they exist only in the mishmashed mind of the writer, but if such thinking should spread, our country will be in more trouble than it now is. It is this kind of incomprehensible letter than first drew me into writing answers, for such thinking needs loud and clear refutation.)

2013, January 3rd, The Record

From: *The Record*, December 16

The argument:

The writer considers all convicts to be equally dangerous to society, and so supports the death penalty. He argues that possible execution of someone innocent is not persuasive, since this rarely if ever occurs. Execution, then, is mandatory, lest some of the killers escape.

2013

From: *The Record,* January 3:

The reply:

Regarding "Death penalty is entirely appropriate" (Your Views, Dec. 16):

Here are a few reasons why it is not.

The letter writer argues that "we have a responsibility to remove evil from the face of the Earth." He would make the convict pure evil, a Satan, which no man ever is. And he would remove him by killing him, thereby committing the same act for which the criminal is being punished. If the felon were Satan, this might be all right but not all killers are "evil"; some are emotionally disturbed, some have acted in momentary rage, some are not yet able to realize the enormity of their crime (there are several cases of such people growing and improving as humans and coming to regret their wrongdoing, something which we would prevent by killing them at once).

Second, the letter writer's confidence that there is "little or no chance of executing an innocent person" is sadly misplaced. In the last few years we have become increasingly uneasy about our legal system, realizing (often through the DNA the writer mentions) that we have imprisoned and in many cases executed innocent people. Formerly "foolproof" evidence like eyewitness identifications or fingerprinting has been shown to be prey to monstrous error, condemning to death those innocent of crime.

Finally he fears that if we don't kill killers, they "could escape." Well, yes, but this possibility is rare, especially for murderers, and there are so many reasons not to kill that this is not sufficient reason for execution; one of these is that it costs more than life imprisonment. And by eliminating the death penalty, we avoid wrongful execution, give the sinner a chance to repent, and punish him more severely by lifelong confinement than by ending his life. The realization of this grows more obvious to us, with more and more states accepting it. It's time to cease senseless defense of capital punishment and make justice more effective and more merciful.

Richard Lettis

(Another important reason for ending the death penalty is its effect upon mind-set of the executioners--who are, in a sense, all of us. That we can coolly wipe a human being (however wicked his offense) out of existence contributes to the indifference to the suffering of others. There is but one justification for any killing and that is as the last act of self-defense.)

Richard Lettis, Ph.D

2013, February 24th, The Record

From: *The Record*, February 17:
Right to life and right to die
The argument:
Regarding "Assembly panel tackles right to end one's life" (Page
A-4, Feb. 8):
"It was with surprise, dismay and disgust," the letter says,
"that I read about how the Assembly Health Committee voted, 7-2, to
move a bill that, if approved by voters, would allow terminally ill
patients the right to end their lives." The bill's name, she notes has
been "sanitized" as the New Jersey Death with Dignity Act, which is
merely another name for legal assisted suicide; it is just the same as
calling an abortion a "procedure." She remarks that the hospice, an
alternate to suicide, "offers compassionate and dignified care for
both the patient and the family." And "No one has the right to play
God and determine when life begins and ends." If supporters of this
bill claim that people have a "right to die," then they should fight
just as hard for a baby's "right to life, for "you can't have it both
ways."

From: *The Record*, February 24:
The reply:
I must respond to the letter writer (Feb. 17, 2013) who argues
that we humans have no right to end our own lives. She appears to
believe that only the physically ill desire to do so, and urges
consulting a hospice instead. But this is over-simplification: there
are many reasons why we may feel compelled to end our lives, and
narrow is the mind that denies all such sufferers the right to end
their pain, of whatever kind, in any and all instances.

As is so often the case on matters of morality, religion is invoked. The writer says, "Absolutely no one has the right to play God and determine when life begins and ends." Which is to say that all who suffer agony of body or mind must wait until the deity decides to be merciful, a thing which He is not known to do frequently, and possibly never happens.

And the letter becomes somewhat confusing in its conclusion, which argues that if we defend the right to die then we must also defend the right of a fetus to live. Does this mean the writer will accept suicide if we all agree to end abortion? And are these two "rights" really the same? Are not the consequences, for instance, quite different from each other? The decision to abort involves another being (in progress), while suicide is a decision that one makes for oneself and carries out upon oneself. Granted, some people decide to die in a moment of temporary despair, but this only means that we need to place the process of self-induced dying in the hands of physicians, who would help sufferers to make a decision, judge their ability to make such a decision, and assist in the least unpleasant method of dying.

Would such a practice be open to flaws? Would some regrettable and even evil treatment sometimes occur? Undoubtedly, but this is true of all human activity. If we tolerated only the completely safe and successful action, none of us would drive cars.

Richard Lettis

Richard Lettis, Ph.D

2013, March 18th, The Record

From: *The Record*, March 14: Gun owners simply want protection

The argument:

Regarding "What laws do gun owners want?" (Your Views, March 9):

It is suggested that "it would be prudent to think that many gun owners want guns to protect themselves and their families." That is especially so when the economy tanks and there is unrest. The police won't save you if they are busy elsewhere. It would be foolhardy not to have protection." With so much violence in our society, "the question is: Who is responsible for one's safety? Who is responsible for your family's safety? But most importantly, who can be held liable and accountable for your family's safety?" In such a dangerous society, "Our lawmakers shouldn't criminalize legitimate gun owners while the criminal elements in our society flout our existing laws." That's the point of the Second Amendment: "to protect us from a tyrannical government."

From: *The Record*, March 18:

The reply:

Regarding "Gun owners simply want protection" (Your Views, March 14):

The letter writer may well be right when he says that many owners "simply want guns to protect themselves." But to say that begins a long and complicated discussion.

First, how much protection do guns provide, and at what cost?

I assume no owner keeps a loaded gun in an unlocked drawer by his bed. That would mean that if he needed it, he must turn on his light, get the key, unlock the drawer and load his pistol, by which time the burglar probably has fled. Then, too, statistics show that far more people in a house with guns die of accident, error or rage than at the hands of an intruder.

I remember one sad incident in which a father killed his daughter when he came home because she had leapt out of a closet to surprise him; as she died, she said, "I love you, Daddy." Is that, or a similar possibility, worth being armed for a burglar who in all probability may never come?

I assume the writer opposes new gun laws. But they are not envisioned to forbid pistols, only assault rifles that kill dozens, usually, it seems, of schoolchildren. Will the writer not at least agree that an assault weapon is not needed to protect a house?

And finally, the letter notes that "the Founding Fathers gave us our Second Amendment rights to protect us from a tyrannical government." Exactly; they did not speak of a possible house intruder. And they wrote more than 200 years ago, when one put a bullet in his rifle, loaded it with gunpowder and tamped it down, before he could shoot. If they were told about a weapon that could fire 100 bullets before reloading, and if they understood that 2,000 men with assault rifles were on their way to Washington to fight the government, my guess is they would have not worded the amendment as they did.

The feel of a gun in one's hand is enticing, the sense of power and safety comforting. But everything about our world now shows that it is too dangerous and delusional. Change is the nature of existence, and what was written long ago must be carefully considered, lest it prove to be a danger today.

Richard Lettis

(The competence of some gun advocates is perhaps shown by a letter in *The Record*, in which the writer mocked me for assuming no one would keep his gun in an unlocked drawer. She is right in arguing that doing so would make shooting the burglar somewhat easier, but sadly wrong in approval of leaving a loaded weapon available to anyone, especially the child who decides to play with it.)

Richard Lettis, Ph.D

2013, April 15th, The Record

From: *The Record*, article, April 15:

The argument:

The writer speaks of "renewed arguments by some federal and state leaders to change the definition of marriage to include same-sex couples. Recent polls reporting increased public support for same-sex marriage have emboldened their push." There is "a creeping cultural shift" engendered by "years of emotional portrayals of same-sex relationships in TV sitcoms, movies and now in blatant advertising campaigns." A Pew Research poll shows that the main reason for 32 percent of those who changed their minds and accept same-sex "marriage" is that they know someone who is gay. It is compassion for the individual that has changed their minds, but "marital ideals and standards that encourage society to aspire to the best possible outcomes cannot be abandoned to accommodate every individual." Other laws, like speeding, are enforced even if some unfortunate soul has to catch an important flight, nor are orchestral standards waived for a musician because he has limited himself to the studying of one instrument and has a family to support. The maintaining of the ideal man-woman definition of marriage, which is "our most important social institution" -- is either right or it is not, and we must not allow our decision to be influenced by compassion for a gay, "whether he is our child, a sibling, friend or anyone else." New Jersey already grants same-sex couples equal benefits under civil-union law, and these unions are commendable for good reason. "A new gold-standard, peer-reviewed, family structures study released in June 2012 by sociology professor Mark Regnerus from the University of Texas indicates that the social experiment of homosexual "marriage" will cause serious harm to children." Children with gay and lesbian parents are more likely than those in a two-parent heterosexual home "to have social and mental health problems requiring therapy, and to identify themselves as homosexual, choose cohabitation in which partners are unfaithful. Same-sex couples are more likely to catch sexually transmitted diseases, to be sexually molested or raped by a parent or adult, to have lower income levels, and to get drunk and smoke tobacco and marijuana.

This study differs from all others in that, the writer says, "it uses a data set of 2,988 persons ages 18 to 39 -- including 175 adults raised by lesbian mothers and 73 adults raised by gay fathers -- marking the first research from a new dataset, which initially included some 15,000 people." The research showed a major difference between children from both groups and that family instability is a "characteristic mark" of same-sex relationships. "These poor life outcomes will require greater government tax dollar assistance and encourage more young people to accept and experiment with same-sex behavior."

Individuals who support the changing of the definition of marriage should remember the social mistakes already made, and are about to make again, which will hurt children most heavily. "They are the innocent victims of social experimentation and have become morally and even physically broken in the name of so-called "'freedom, equality and progress.'" Since 1994, homosexuality of men has increased 18 percent, but of women it has increased 157 percent, which suggests strong cultural factors encouraging same-sex behaviors. At least indirectly, this confutes the theory of "being "'born that way.'"

A gay man, Doug Mainwaring, has written wrote an insightful article for the publicdiscourse.com. His intellectual honesty and experience as a gay person raising children supports the opposing of same-sex marriage. He says that "There are perhaps a hundred different things, small and large, that are negotiated between parents and kids every week. . . . Moms and dads interact differently with their children. To give kids two moms or two dads is to withhold ... someone whom they desperately need and deserve in order to be whole and happy. It is to permanently etch 'deprivation' on their hearts."

(Toni Meyer is Sr. Research Analyst, NJ Family Policy Council)

From: *The Record*, April:

The reply:

The attempt of Toni Meyer ("Why we should not redefine marriage") to convince us that gay marriage is bad for children has served only to illustrate how desperate the opposition has become in its effort to prevent two people who love each other from marrying.

Judging from the angry letters* recently printed in The Record, Meyer has stepped into a hornet's nest. These letters properly focus upon Meyer's use of Mark Regnerus's faulty study, which concludes that the children of gay marriage are damaged, both morally and physically. One letter mentions the criticism of Regnerus by Social Science Research, to which may be added another important study by the American Sociological Association, which summed up its thorough examination of Regnerus with a conclusion that should leave no doubt concerning its authenticity: "by conflating children raised by same sex parents with individuals who reportedly had a parent who had 'a romantic relationship with someone of the same sex,' and referring to such individuals as children of 'lesbian mothers' or 'gay fathers,' the Regnerus study obscures the fact that it did not specifically examine children raised by two same-sex parents. Accordingly, it cannot speak to the impact of same-sex parents on child outcomes."

The anti-gay forces have repeatedly used the work of Rengerus to support their argument, but in so doing have placed themselves directly in the crosshairs of criticism. Either they have not been aware of its faults, and so are guilty of poor research, or they have known its bad reputation and have committed the unethical act of using it anyway. To the decimation of Regnerus may be added additional examination of Meyer's argument. The first indication that something is wrong occurs as early as the second paragraph, in which she employs a loaded word (an expression that defines, but also expresses prejudice against, an object). She says that the television and movie stories about gays give us "emotional portrayals," as opposed, apparently, to heterosexual stories, which do not. And the many writings in defense of gay marriage are described as "blatant advertising campaigns," apparently to be contrasted with the opposition to gay marriage, which, unlike Meyer's own work, is always quiet and inoffensive.

Then comes the argument. "Marital ideals and standards that encourage society to aspire for the best possible outcomes cannot be abandoned to accommodate every individual." First, the question of what the best possible outcomes are must be discussed in detail (with, possibly, no final agreement). Second, part of the greatness of our country is that it has always endeavored (when at its best) to consider the needs of the individual, not passing laws that prevent a single person from possessing the rights of our Constitution.

Meyer says that "we must not base our decision on compassion for gays (or misunderstood sense of fairness) whether the gay individual is our child, sibling, friend or anyone else." There is an insensitivity here, in troublesome contrast to her concern for the welfare of children who "are the innocent victims of social experimentation who have become morally and even physically broken in the name of so-called 'freedom, equality and progress.'" Which is to say that a father learns that his beloved son is gay, and rejects him; weep for your boy, Dad, but have nothing more to do with him.

We may note that the children of heterosexual marriages also sometimes suffer damage from the many intricacies of two adults attempting to live together and, being human, make mistakes in parenting. As for morality, Meyer would have us accept her version of it without any explanation of why it is wrong for two people of the same sex to love each other and wish to marry. And again, the evidence of physical damage to which she refers simply does not exist.

Finally, the writer cites the increase of homosexuality in men at 18 percent and women at 157 percent. This, she says, "clearly suggests that there are strong cultural factors at work in encouraging same-sex behaviors and that, at least indirectly, it undermines the whole theory of 'being born that way.'" Her point is that the cultural change has produced homosexuals who would have, without it, been heterosexual. She seems to be unaware that until recently the admission of homosexuality had had its dangers, and that in all likelihood we do not have more homosexuals than before, just more who now feel safe enough to declare their sexual orientation. Should Meyer and company restore us to the time when gays were confined to closets, they would have the pleasure of seeing the number of admitted gays decline again. And we note that Meyer has come out of her own particular closet: not only should gays not be parents, they should not be gay. The conclusion that must be reached after reading this article is that the anti-gay contingent grows increasingly desperate as the unstoppable wave of the gay movement progresses. Having apparently accepted the fact that the "it has always been, and so must always be" argument , is at last dismissed not only as groundless but as foolish, the adherence of the opposition to same-sex marriage is reduced to unsubstantiated studies and illogical arguments, and to a certain coldness toward the welfare of a good portion of our population.

Richard Lettis

2013, April 2nd, The Record

From: *The Record,* April 2:

(A subsequent letter disagreed, arguing that I had made "an inaccurate critique of research regarding greater pathologies in children of homosexual parents, conducted by respected sociology professor Mark Regnerus of the University of Texas." His work, he said, had "been reaffirmed as valid and without misrepresentation." The data was "based upon surveys from young adult children of homosexual parents rather than parents themselves.")

A similar study in Holland, he argued, supported the Regnerus study, finding that "the divorce rate for homosexual marriages is 80 percent and most of the spouses had six to eight extra-marital affairs during their one-and-one-half year marriages." This research was made by the Netherlands Study on Gay Marriage by Maria Xiridou, which, since we know nothing about the lady, does sound impressive.

The writer also claimed that domestic violence in homosexual relationships is much higher than heterosexual ones, which made it "not inconceivable that children raised in this type of environment could have greater incidents of pathology." "What I find most telling, he concludes, "comes from the mouths of homosexual activists themselves. According to journalist Masha Gessen, "We lie that the institution of marriage is not going to change. The institution of marriage is going to change. I don't think it should exist. I have three kids who have five parents and I don't see why they shouldn't have five parents legally."

From: *The Record,* April:

The reply:

This strikes me as a rather weak conclusion: to end with an assertion is of no value unless evidence to support it is given (and it is not). The Netherlands Study has come under severe criticism, for example, that "the study had nothing to do with relationships; it was conducted by Dr. *Maria Xiridou* to find out how AIDS was transferring in a community." Maria Xiridou's report seems to parallel that of Regnerus, used by those who oppose gay marriage and reviled by all others. Masha Gessen is a respectable author and reporter, but questionable as a reliable commentator on gay marriage and children. On the other hand, William Meezan, who holds a chair at Fordham University, and Jonathan Rouch, a senior fellow at Brookings Institute, conducted a study of all research to date and concluded that "the children who have been studied are doing about as well as children normally do." And I may add Child Trends to the list of organizations which refute the charges leveled by Regnerus.)

From: *The Record,* July:

Gun clip limits don't save lives

The argument: (stated in reply)

From: *The Record,* July:

The Reply:

The question of why a gun owner needs a magazine containing an excessive number of rounds is, the writer says, "a dirty trick designed to win the gun control debate without thought." From what planet has he recently returned?

The bodies of children strewn on the floors of their classrooms, some of whom would not have died if the madman had been obliged to reload, do indeed create emotion, but they also produce an undeniable thought: limit the size of a magazine and lives will be saved. And to accuse the earnest and anguished presenters of this conviction as "trying a dirty trick" is abominable.

The writer next gets lost in his own argument. "By explaining why I would need a standard-capacity magazine, I allow the questioner to turn the entire debate around," he says. But what would the debate be without the question and his answer (which he never gives)? Now, he moans, "I have to go to the government to ask permission for something." Permission for what? If the attempted ban on such magazines is defeated he, does not have to go to anyone; if it is passed, he cannot get permission from anyone. The argument is dissolving in senselessness.

The writer concludes with the assertion that he has the right to carry enough bullets to slay a large body of people, a "right . . . for an overriding common good." Can he provide a single instance in which the firing of a hundred rounds by a civilian has resulted in good for anybody? As we know all too well, there is a painful plethora of instances on the other side.

Richard Lettis

(The issue in the following letter was whether stores should be closed on Sundays. Probably when first so ordered, the consideration was religious, but for some time now the real argument has been that it is a good idea to reduce traffic and help Sunday travelers get around.

Richard Lettis, Ph.D

2013, August 17th, The Record

From: *The Record*, August 14:
Country blue laws respect the Sabbath
The argument:

In the debate about whether Bergen County's blue laws should be voided, those who support the proposal "often say that it is a matter of convenience to shop in department stores, buy cars or whatever on Sundays." But the writer of this letter says she believes there is "more at stake than our puny convenience." She argues that society today "is so enslaved by a compulsion to 'have' and to 'buy' that any day on which we cannot do so with unfettered liberty is now viewed as dreadful" by those consumers who are impatient for more chances to shop. She asks if we are ready to confess as a society that we no longer believe there is a God, or that he has no right to establish commandments to be observed. "We are still a vastly Judeo-Christian civilization, and the Ten Commandments are clearly established." The commandment about keeping the Sabbath holy intended to create a day "on which all profane activities would be set aside, and she says she feels a relief "to experience the cessation of the non-stop buying and selling, the escalating consumerism that is suffocating the higher nature of man, and to see - in contrast - the relative stillness of the Sabbath." She feels respect for a Jewish Community Center which closes on Saturdays to observe the Jewish Sabbath, though that is probably the day when most athletic equipment is purchased.

"If we hope to have God's blessing and protection in the increasingly difficult days with which we are faced, we must stop insulting him and disregarding his reasonable and healthy requests, of which keeping the Sabbath is but one."

From: *The Record*, August 17:

Regarding "County blue laws respect the Sabbath" (Other Views, Aug. 14):

The reply:

The writer is subject to the same misunderstanding as those who cry that we must "keep Christ in Christmas."

No one is trying to force Christians to remove Jesus from that holiday, or to shop on Sunday. The issue is whether Christians have the right to prevent the rest of us (and there are more and more of us in what he calls the "vastly Judeo-Christian" society") from enjoying the holiday as we see fit and shopping when we want.

Those who do not believe in the Christian God (or do not consider the Bible as the director of their lives) do His worshippers no harm in spending Sunday in any legitimate way they wish. And the suggestion that in so doing we lose "God's blessing" does not, in light of the fact that believers do not fare any better than we unblessed, cause us concern.

Let the religious of all faiths conduct their lives as they think fit. Let the non-religious do the same.

Richard Lettis

Richard Lettis, Ph.D

2014, January 1st, The Record

From: *The Record*, December 25:

Christmas editorial overlooked key fact regarding "Seeking harmony" (Editorials):

The argument:

The writer gave notice that Dec. 25 had been Christmas, "the day that Christians all over the world celebrate the birth of Jesus Christ, the son of God." Believing that God "became flesh and dwelt among" us so we might know him and his great love, Christians celebrate this gift on Christmas Day. But The Record's editorial "did not even remotely touch on the meaning of Christmas," focusing instead on not offending non-Christians: "You wrote, 'Out of respect for others, we are careful about saying it is Christmas Day.'" The writer asks whether the editor has written the same thing about such holidays as Hanukah, Ramadan and Kwanzaa. "Each of those observances are celebrated by a particular group of people. What others do on Christmas Day is their business. But that does not change the significance of the day for us as Christians".

From: *The Record,* December 22:

The argument:

The writer criticizes an editorial in *The Record* which she believes attempted to make the significance of Christmas seen in another way.

2014

From: *The Record*, January 1:

Regarding "Christmas editorial overlooked key fact" (Your Views, Dec. 27):

The argument: See replying letter.

From: *The Record,* January:

The reply:

Here is still another mistaken letter regarding Christ in Christmas, but this time the argument focuses solely on Christians; it ends with the statement that "what others do on Christmas Day is their business."

The writer complains because *The Record's* editorial "did not even remotely touch on the meaning of Christmas." But *The Record's* editorial in no way tried, as the writer asserts, to "change the significance of the day for us as Christians." In short, the writer's point seemed to be that it's OK to do what *The Record* wanted to do, unless it wanted to speak of something other than the Christian meaning of Christmas. Does this make sense? All the objectors need to do is not read the editorial, and leave it to those who want to read it.

This and similar letters disclose a kind of religious egotism: what the writers want must be done by everybody or they are offended. It is time to accept the fact, as the editorial indicates, that non-Christians owe no homage or extra attention to the complainers' religious beliefs. *The Record* was simply trying for the benefit of all to write on a holiday without confinement to any single belief. Let's have it that way.

(Note too the illogic: The editorial was for all, including those non-Christians she speaks of; if she allows them their own way of celebrating, why should not the editorial (*The Record* is not a religious publication) write for them as well as for Christians?)

Richard Lettis

Richard Lettis, Ph.D

2014, February 9th, The Record

From: *The Record*, February 4:

The argument:

Guns are vital to nation's security

The writer argues that "like it or not, an armed citizenry is crucial to our nation's survival." And though he recognizes that "many argue that times have changed and the Second Amendment is outdated," he "find[s] it most interesting that our leaders in Washington, many of whom have vowed to disarm our citizens, are the same leaders agreeing to supply small arms and other weaponry" to other countries. He finds it "logical to think that if the Syrian people had been allowed to own guns in the first place . . . their government might not have become so tyrannical." And he concludes that "the United States wouldn't be supplying the rebels with guns and ammunition if we didn't believe that guns could effectively solve the problem, balance power, and alleviate their oppression."

From: *The Record*, February 9:

Regarding "Guns are vital to nation's security" (Your Views, Feb. 4):

The reply:

The writer argues that since our government is supplying weapons to the Syrian rebels, it should also permit American citizens to be equally armed in case they too decide to rebel. One problem with this idea is seen in the writer's positing that the weapons given to us would have to be "similar to those available to the Syrian military," meaning that if we decided to overthrow our government, we would need, among other things, howitzers, antiaircraft weapons, bazookas, tanks, and fighter planes (our armed forces are superior to those of Syria). This, of course, means that we would need the money to purchase these weapons, and several million citizens to use them. In addition to America's present military, many citizens who would support the government would enlist, making our army formidable opponents indeed.

In truth, the writer's fondness for the Second Amendment's statement that citizens should have the right to bear arms causes him to fail to understand that it was made in a time quite different from ours. The writers of the amendment were concerned that, in a newly born country, that which history shows has happened in similar nations might happen to them, and so they wished to provide means by which, if their government attempted to become tyrannical, armed citizens would be able to oppose it.

The nation's militia then was small, small enough to be defeated. But now it is not, and we are still a democracy. And no matter how much a relatively few citizens believe, in the face of all evidence, that President Obama is a tyrant, they are a minority, and their rebellion would be like David and Goliath, but David with no sling shot.

Richard Lettis

Richard Lettis, Ph.D

2014, May 24th, The Record

From: *The Record*, May11:

The argument:

(This essay is very long, and somewhat fragmentary; I have paraphrased and quoted the most important points only.)

Sex between adult and teenager has received much attention, often discussed with a tolerant attitude. The crime is "underreported, experts say, in part because of that entrenched stereotype that the boy in such cases is not so much victim but victor," the thought being that "young men being with older women is a desirable thing, like in 'The Graduate,' " A psychologist Linda Centeno said that "It's not seen so much as abuse as an actual relationship. ... It's almost as if boys are taught they should feel like there's something cool about this."

Teenage girls, however, "react very differently than boys in such situations." They may at first feel fortunate: they are in love, but if the man is caught, "she is then dealing with the fact that she's been victimized," especially since "females are socialized to be victims in society in general." But "Male students , , , do not automatically get labeled as victims, and may not even feel that it applies." They may be admired by other youths, but, as with girls, if the adult women are arrested and sentenced, they are criticized, because they have "got the teacher in trouble." In any case, "it may take men years to realize that they're a victim, if they ever do". These differences in reaction have "affected how society has traditionally viewed them." There is now "a better understanding of sexual abuse . . . [of] . . . girls, but we haven't developed that as much for boys and men." The executive director of Male Survivor has said that "In our culture men are supposed to be invulnerable. They aren't supposed to talk about it." Another influential factor is "whether or not the teenager feels like he's been abused rather than part of a willing relationship or encounter." Because "males are seen as dominant and aggressive, their part in an affair with an adult woman "is automatically interpreted as inappropriate and unjust." Females, on the other hand, "are seen as caring and giving, which is incompatible with the idea of being selfish or aggressive in a sexual way."

It is a myth that the boy must have enjoyed the affair and so feels that it is being taken from him. Adult males sometimes wish they had enjoyed such a relationship. A judge who voiced this opinion and merely sentenced the accused woman to probation without jail time was reprimanded "for controversial comments," and another judge sentenced the woman to three years in prison. The conviction now is that "these situations are crimes of power, not acts of passion," a Mahwah resident said. The article then turns to a consideration of the politics of rape. Before the 1970s, "a woman and an underage male did not legally qualify as statutory rape in most states." There were no "national associations for male sexual-abuse victims," and some films "glamorized having sex with older women." Several cases of adult-child relations are examined. Experts say that situations depicting acceptable sex of this kind distort a larger picture. There are some cases in which the boy marries the teacher and they claim everything's fine, but that's a rare occurrence": "Even if a boy says it's something like a conquest, there's still a boundary being crossed and that person is still a victim," an expert who treats young sexual-abuse victims has said. "It's confusing, it's secret, it's wrong, it's illegal, and the effects are more damaging than what society would have us believe."

From: *The Record*, May 24:

Regarding "School sex cases where victim is seen as victor" (Page

A-1, May 11):

The reply:

It is encouraging to see that an increasing number of people have expressed doubt about the supposed harmful effect on teenagers of their having sex with an adult.

The Record has covered a number of these legal offenses, reporting that several adults are now serving jail terms for them. Some of these may deserve punishment, but the concern has never received the kind of careful thinking through that it needs, perhaps because, though we have made considerable strides in our attitude toward sex, the Puritan distrust and fear of sexuality still impedes clear-headed thinking.

Charges leveled against adults who have violated the relevant law usually give two explanations: the adult has "contributed to the delinquency of," and/or "endangered the welfare of" the teenager. There is, of course, possible harm in any sexual relationship, but what reason is there to believe that teenage-adult sex really causes unusual damage to anyone?

If an attractive adult woman had taken me to her bed when I was 16, I would still be blessing her name. Unless someone can supply convincing evidence that a teenager, whom nature has prepared for sexual activity, is in any way harmed, the idea that youngsters should be protected from what we, after all, call "love-making" needs to be eradicated, and the people serving time for the purported crime should be freed.

Does this hold true for girls as well as boys? Not quite, because while the boy has no more to lose than anyone else engaged in sex, the girl does: teenage pregnancy can, of course, engender serious consequences. But we have several means of avoiding pregnancy today, and so the only man who should be sent to jail for bedding a consenting minor is someone who fails to take the necessary precautions.

That men and women should now be imprisoned for an act never proved to be harmful must be of serious concern for us all. We must dismiss the idea that so many aspects of our sexuality are suspect. This gimpy idea that the sex act is deeply suspect goes as far back at least as the Apostle Paul, and will not be erased without vigorous contention from more and more guilt-free and sensible people.

Richard Lettis

(My Roman Catholic daughter has informed me that, because teenagers are not yet old enough to understand all factors concerning sex, it is harmful for them to engage in sex with an adult. Indeed, she said, premarital sex will hurt the individuals, both mentally and physically. She claimed that several authorities had reached this decision. I looked up what was available, and found that all of these authorities are Catholic. More than says that during the act of sex dopamine is released in the brain; while this may be of benefit to a married person, it is in some way (I found no explanation of how) unhealthy for those who are not married. This conviction seems to me to come not from scientific investigation (I found no writer who explained in detail why a physical act such as sex could be beneficial in one situation and harmful in another), but from that prejudice against sexuality that goes back at least as far as the letter-writing Paul of the Bible, who warned all against it, reluctantly accepting marital sex because total avoidance does burn, and we obviously can't get on without it. Catholics — and, granted, some others — find they are losing if they try to prevent sex as sinful, and are falling back upon contracted assertions of damage not so much to the soul is to the body — we see this same kind of argument in the attempts to ban same-sex marriage because, it is claimed, children are harmed by it.)

Richard Lettis, Ph.D

2014, April 5th, The Record

From: *The Record*, March:

The argument:

"Religious freedom is intrinsically linked to our freedom as individuals, as well as our country's founding and laws . . . a most treasured right that must be protec**t**ed above all if a society is to remain free," the letter proclaims. The Bill of Rights guarantees this; "the right to live according to one's own faith, manifesting that religion or belief in practice . . . without interference from the state." And there is nothing in the First Amendment that makes any "distinction between living out our religious beliefs in church versus the 'secular' world." But that freedom is now under fire, with "New laws that have created special privileges for sexual orientation and gender identity [which] are being used to trump our fundamental free exercise of religion." Businesses — especially those which serve in some way weddings--"have been increasingly hauled into court and sued for declining to provide services for a same-sex ceremony that they view as a violation of their faith." And court rulings "have not only ignored and subjugated people's basic religious freedom by calling liberty discrimination, they have punished Christians in particular with steep fines, or cost them their business." The goal, as a state official put it, is to "rehabilitate," which simply means obliging Christians to change their beliefs. But instead of rehabilitation, "what the owners of Sweet Cakes experienced was ridicule, vicious protests, boycotts and death threats to their family of five." In New Jersey there have been two first challenges to religious freedom regarding property and business, and given the "political landscape, they won't be the last." A Camp Association "was forced to either allow a lesbian civil union on their boardwalk pavilion or give up their tax-exempt status for that property," and a dating business "was forced to accommodate gay online dating matches to remain in business in New Jersey." LGBT activists, government officials, and judges who say that, "Americans should be free to live and love as they choose without fear of government sanction" are forcing everyone to "agree with them and celebrate it -- or else." In this they are subverting the law, saying, "You can live out your religion in churches - but not in the public square." That people know this is wrong is attested by the polls: In a Rasmussen poll, "85 percent said they think a Christian has a right to turn down a same-sex wedding job." And "those in the LGBT community who are honest know it is wrong." Under this law, "a homosexual painter [would] be forced to paint signs for the infamous Westboro Baptist Church in Topeka that reads 'God Hates Fags!' In defense of religious freedom,"18 states have passed religious-freedom restoration laws, to clearly restore our foundational freedoms under fire. These laws are based on the federal 1993 Religious Freedom Restoration Act, which states: The federal government 'shall not substantially burden a person's exercise of religion' unless it can demonstrate that such a burden 'is in furtherance of a compelling governmental interest; and 'is the least restrictive means of furthering that compelling interest.'" Another attack on religious freedom is in The Patient Protection and Affordable Care Act abortion-pill mandate, which is "determined to force people of faith to abandon their belief or face crippling fines." Two companies are challenging the mandate that would force them to pay for abortion-inducing drugs, which is more than the "fundamental contraception," which headlines claim. "Under the Constitution, the government has no right telling individuals to check their religious values at the door in vast areas of human life such as business or health care." We are urged to support religious liberty legislation and to elect representatives "who will again secure our right to religious liberty and conscience." For "if religious liberty was denied these citizens, how long before it is taken from you?"

Len Deo is executive director of the New Jersey Family Policy Council.

From: *The Record*, April 5:

The reply:

Regarding "Reinforcement of religious-freedom protections needed" (March 28):

Columnist Len Deo argues that religion needs more protection of its right to exercise its principles. Let us see.

First, freedom of anything is necessarily restricted. My freedom to cut down trees does not permit me to trespass on your yard and cut down yours. Often, one kind of freedom impinges upon another, and when this happens we must decide which freedom is more important.

The question here is whether the freedom to believe that homosexuality is a sin is more important than the civil rights of gays. A person serving a gay individual may not like to do so, but his opinion is obviously less important than the right of his customer to marry someone he loves and still shop anywhere for anything he pleases.

In any case, Deo's "photographers, bakers, florists" should not refuse to serve individuals who are gay unless they also deny any customer who violates their other religious convictions. They must ask each person if he obeys the Ten Commandments, does not swear, believes that Jesus Christ is his savior, and so on. All of which means that religious freedom, if fully and honestly used, cannot justify refusal to serve.

No one is attempting to "force people of faith to abandon their belief." Rather, the intent is to assure the rights of everyone to be treated equally. I do not know if Deo is a Catholic, but whether he is or not, he should take a lesson from Pope Francis: "Who am I to judge?"

Richard Lettis

(The acceptance of homosexuality has grown from negative to positive in a time shorter than almost any other group, and judges in state after state have ruled a ban on gay marriage to be unconstitutional. By the time this note is read, the Supreme Court will have decided whether a national acceptance of this marriage becomes law. From all signs to this date, hope for this decision is high.)

2014, May 17th, The Record

From: *The Record*, May 9:

No college for inmates. Regarding "Governor promotes college for inmates" (Page A-3, May 9):

The argument:

The writer asks why a convicted felon should be given an education. He points out that while convicts were committing their crimes, "against the taxpayers of New Jersey," some of their peers were working hard--"long hours and long days," and giving up much to stay in school. "And what do they have to show for their efforts?" he asks. When they graduate, many of them, who have incurred large debts which they now have to try to pay back, find it difficult to find work in New Jersey. Are they given any help? Why should felons be rewarded for their bad conduct and crimes against society, while "many of our own children struggle to move forward from their monetary educational debt burden?" He wonders if he is the only one who is disturbed by the governor's "thought process." It "just seems a bit too much, when many of us teach our children to be self-sufficient and to be productive citizens." He approves of rehabilitation, but argues that the felon should be required to pay the same money as do our children to be educated, "and not be another entitlement, as our governor likes to say."

From: *The Record*, May 17:

The reply:

A skeptical writer (May 9) asks, "Why would anyone give an education to a convicted felon?" Let us see if we can find an answer.

The difference between a penitentiary and hell is that the words "Abandon all hope ye who enter here" are not written over the entrance to the former. The damned have no hope because they are intrinsically wicked and will not or cannot change. It is true that some convicts are similar, but also that some are different.

Some men and women in jail simply made a terrible mistake, or succumbed to a powerful temptation, or have lived under such circumstances that they have felt driven to crime. These individuals are capable of regeneration, and while some will fail in the attempt, all deserve a chance. If when they are freed they are unprepared — have been so treated in prison that they have lost all self-respect, and must seek employment while stained with their record of conviction, and incapable of doing any work that requires an education — the chances of their returning to criminal ways is greatly increased. And any possible capacity for good and useful work must be lost.

And if we grant that those in jail are still human and that, though they must pay for their crimes by the loss of liberty, they still deserve the right to live without the disastrous effects of remaining in ignorance and the pain of knowing that society has abandoned them. Such people may become desperate; their lives will be, indeed, a kind of hell. And any one of us may be their victim. I believe that the wise and compassionate Jesus would, if apprised of this situation, say something about casting stones.

Richard Lettis

(Readers may be interested in the government action against which the writer protested.)

GOVERNOR PROMOTES COLLEGE FOR INMATES

HEARS HOW STATE PROGRAM HELPED CHANGE LIVES

One was picked up on drug charges. Another served time for robbery. A third for shooting a woman with a BB gun.

171

The former inmates who sat around a table with Governor Christie at Mercer County Community College on Thursday all had different circumstances that led them to a program that helped them transition from prison to higher education - an opportunity they all say has put them on a better path and one Christie was there to promote.

"My life has completely changed," said Amarilis Rodriguez, a Camden native now living in Jersey City. "I am no long stifling my potential. I'm planning on applying to grad school, and my biggest goal is to be able to give back to my community in some way or another."

Rodriguez was sentenced to 30 months in prison on drug possession and distribution charges at age 26. She never thought about pursuing a college degree until an academic adviser at the Newark halfway house told her about a program. Now at 35, she has a bachelor's degree in women's and gender studies and information technology from Rutgers University, and she is working with at-risk youth at a non-profit in New York.

Christie was in West Windsor on Thursday to announce an expansion of that program -- New Jersey Scholarship and Transformative Education in Prison, or NJ-STEP. The program, run through a consortium led by Rutgers in partnership with the state of Education and Corrections departments, serves about 500 inmates in six of the state's 13 correctional facilities. Over the next four years, the program will grow to 2,000 inmates in 10 facilities.

Begun in 2012, the program is being expanded through $4 million in grants Rutgers received from the Ford Foundation and the Sunshine Lady Foundation.

"Ninety-five percent of incarcerated men and women will be released and come back to their neighborhoods," said Mitty Beal, executive director of the Sunshine Lady Foundation. "This is a captive audience, and while they're serving their time, it only makes good sense to educate them so they come back more readily prepared to become citizens and good parents, sons and daughters, taxpaying employees - the people that we want them to become and that they want to become also."

Mercer County Community College, Essex County College, Princeton University, Raritan Valley Community College, the College of New Jersey, Drew University and Salem Community College also participate in the program. Professors from the colleges teach courses in the prisons, and counselors help the inmates' transition to institutions of higher education after their release.

Christie, who has pressed an expansion of drug court, making it mandatory for non-violent offenders to get treatment rather than serve time, said everyone needs to be given a chance to live up to their full potential, regardless of circumstances.

"Sometimes we find that potential in a 16-year-old woman sitting in a jail cell addicted to heroin," he said. "Her life is no less precious, nor valuable, nor a gift from God, than the life of that 16-year-old student whose potential is so obvious that it blinds you. We need to make sure that we bring that message to everyone, and through programs like this, we're beginning to be able to do that."

Steven Hauck, 27, of Egg Harbor Township spent 28 months in prison on weapons possession. He earned 33 credits through the NJ-STEP program and enrolled in Atlantic Cape Community College within days of his release in December thanks to the help of an adviser who continues to check on him.

"You can be vulnerable in prison," he said. "There's not much to grasp onto, so when there's an opportunity like that, you can really grab onto it, and that's what happened and the NJ-STEP program."

Khalil Lockett of Newark told the governor he was released three weeks ago after serving five years at three different correctional facilities for robbery and resisting arrest. Lockett earned 27 credits while he was incarcerated and enrolled in Raritan Valley Community College with the help of his adviser. He hopes to go to business school at Rutgers next year and said the program has changed his life.

"This helped me not have to worry about going back and repeating the same thing," Lockett said. "This opportunity, it widens what I can do."

2014, June 29th, The Record

From: *The Record*, June 11:

Atheists can't rival the Pope

The argument:

"Atheists, the writer asserts, "use their venom on Christianity in an effort to drive religion out of the public square . . . often mocking, denigrating and ridiculing all religion. He complains that at Christmas time, "atheist groups paid to put up giant highway billboards in northern New Jersey saying, 'You know it's a myth and you have a choice,' referring to the Christmas narrative," a statement which is "tantamount to hate speech." He charges that atheists "liken their struggle . . . to the gay-rights movement in asking atheists to 'come out of the closet." Also, "They forget that it was Christianity above all else that literally shaped Western civilization."

"Which atheist leader," he wonders, "has the moral authority the pope has," and offers proof: "He just brought together Palestinian President Mahmoud Abbas and Israeli President Shimon Peres not only to pray together with the pontiff, but also to embrace and hold private peace talks at the Vatican. Secular governments have failed to accomplish peace in the Middle East over and over again." Atheists would do well to put up billboards "in hopes of bringing peace to the Mideast."

From: *The Record*, June 29:

Regarding "Atheists can't rival the pope" (Your Views, June 9):

The reply:

It's almost impossible to find anything in this letter that is correct.

"Atheists use their venom on Christianity in an effort to drive religion out of the public square. But do more, often mocking, denigrating and ridiculing all religion." So says the writer.

Ironically, this letter is far more venomous than anything I know of an atheist saying. Perhaps some instances of mocking, denigrating or ridiculing may be found, but at its best atheism seeks only to express its convictions. (This is what was attempted on the billboard the writer condemns.) And expressing the belief that the idea of a deity "is a myth" can hardly be called "hate speech."

The letter goes on to compare the spread of atheism to that of the gays -- to what purpose is a mystery, though there is the uncomfortable suspicion that the idea is to denigrate both.

Atheists "forget that it was Christianity above all else that literally shaped Western civilization." Well, not literally, and by no means is the influence of Christianity forgotten. Most atheists are knowledgeable about religion (the Bible is one of author Richard Dawkins'* favorite books). And while Christianity may be credited with much that it has given to civilization, it must also be criticized for much it has done. Go see the movie "Philomena," about a mother whose child was taken away by the church. Or remember the Spanish Inquisition. Or the religious wars, lasting 30 years, one hundred years. These and far more did some unfortunate shaping.

The writer then wonders "which atheist leader has the moral authority the pope has?" Where has such a question come from? Atheists make no effort to compete with the pope, or the nun next door, in moral or any other kind of authority. And the writer might note that the power of the pope and his church has decreased in the last few decades.

The kind of blind and ferocious hatred of atheism expressed in this letter is inexcusable. It is far better for those of opposing beliefs to talk to each other, preferably with courtesy.

Richard Lettis

(I might have added that the writer's heavy-handed mockery not only fails to further but actually impairs his purpose.)

(*Richard Dawkins, a professor at Oxford, is the author of *The God Delusion*.)

Richard Lettis, Ph.D

2014, July 23rd, The Record

From: *The Record*, July 23:

The argument:

(The following explains the subject upon which the letter-writer comments, and I reply to his letter.)

Governor Christie may be learning that no matter how much traveling he does out of state, it's tough to leave New Jersey issues behind. Visiting Connecticut on Monday in his capacity as head of the Republican Governors Association, Christie was confronted by more than 100 protesters upset with his recent veto of a bill that would have lowered maximum ammunition clip size in New Jersey from 15 rounds to 10.

While gun control is an emotional topic that transcends state lines, some of the anti-Christie passion on this issue can be blamed on the governor himself. In vetoing the bill earlier this month, Christie said it defied common sense and dismissed it as "grandstanding." He also refused to discuss his veto with parents of some of the children killed in the 2012 massacre at Sandy Hook Elementary School in Newtown, Conn.

Commenting further a few days later, the governor belittled those seeking a 10-round ammunition limit by asking, "Why 10? Why not six, why not two, why not one, why not zero?" That was pure political rhetoric. The bill in question called solely for a 10-round limit.

Gun violence is understandably a very real issue in Connecticut. There's nothing abstract about a gunman murdering 26 people, most of whom were small children, in a school. Nor are calls for ammunition limits grandstanding, or worthy of a dismissive response.

Some of the parents of Sandy Hook victims believe their children were killed because gunman Adam Lanza was firing a weapon with a 30-round magazine. Other parents say they think their children may have survived because Lanza eventually had to stop firing to reload.

No one can say with absolute certainty if the parents' assertions are correct, but the governor should have listened to their concerns before he vetoed the bill. His contention that he had previously met with the parents was unpersuasive.

Asked again about the gun limit veto on Monday while visiting a diner, Christie talked about having an "honest disagreement" with protesters.

An honest disagreement is understandable; the governor's dismissive comments upon vetoing the bill were not

From: *The Record*:

Ammo limits would not make us safer. Regarding "Gun-clip limit could save lives" (Your Views, July 18):

The argument:

The letter writer asked, "Why doesn't the governor listen to the electorate who put him into office and sign meaningful legislation to limit the number of rounds in a clip?" He explains why: "Criminals do not follow the law. I do not see what a useless piece of legislation reducing magazine capacity would have done. Criminals can easily purchase or acquire higher-round magazines in other states." To illustrate, he says that the individual who shot Police Officer Melvin Santiago was a criminal, and asks "What would have stopped him from getting a firearm with a higher-capacity magazine had he not forcefully stolen the gun from a security guard?" Does the letter writer upon whom he is commenting] believe that criminals will obey "another useless New Jersey gun restriction" and give up the "above-the-legal-limit gun magazines?" He suggests that, instead of "restricting and turning law-abiding citizens into felons," it would be better to oblige state legislators to deal with the causes of crime and violence rather than pass useless legislation that even they admit would not reduce crime? The writer, a retired sergeant with the Jersey City Police Department, feels sure the letter writer would agree that to consider the roots of crime and violence would achieve better results than "restricting the rights of law-abiding citizens and turning those citizens into felons."

From: *The Record*, July, August:

Gun clip limits don't save lives. Regarding "Christie on guns" (Editorials, July 23):

Second letter (similar argument):

The writer calls the editorial which paid respect to the Sandy Hook school parents in Connecticut who protested Governor Christie's veto of the gun magazine limit a farce. He derides The Record's opinion as "its usual mantra of anti-gun, anti-Second Amendment rhetoric." The paper "has not shown any proof, studies or documents that reducing the size of gun magazines from 15 rounds to 10 rounds would reduce killing by a mentally deranged shooter." It also cites Assemblyman Louis Greenwald, D-Camden, who sponsored the 10-round magazine limit legislation, saying he read studies on the reduction being effective, but declares that he" never produced one study to support his statistics." The writer tells of an Indiana sheriff's department which did a live-fire test which it put on YouTube. The department, he says, "found that it takes 18 seconds to fire off and reload two 15-round magazines, 19 seconds to fire off and reload three 10-round magazines, and 21 seconds to fire off and reload six, five-round magazines." Adam Lanza, the Sandy Hook shooter, fired 30-round magazines but hadn't completely emptied them when he reloaded, which, the writer says, "shows only that he was firing for maximum effect." "Before The Record goes off spouting how Christie vetoed the gun magazine limit bill and dismissed the Sandy Hook parents" he concludes, it should recognize "a Legislature that would have dismissed the rights of thousands of gun owners. Many testified before the legislative committees, but were ignored."

From: *The Record*, July 27:

The argument:

The writer argues against gun-clip limitation because criminals would still easily get larger clips; the law would be impossible to enforce.

From: *The Record*, August:

The reply (to all above letters):

The writer's argument that gun-clip limitation would be "a useless piece of legislation" is faulty. He points out that criminals "do not follow the law," and could "easily purchase or acquire higher-round magazines in other states."

We may suggest that if large clips are illegal, it would not be "easy" for anyone to acquire them. And if we erase every law because criminals do not obey them, we would have few laws left. And a criminal is by definition one who breaks laws, so we should rather expect one would break a limited bullet law, hardly reason to conclude the law would be of no purpose.

We may hope that the limit on gun-clip size would make it harder for criminals to acquire them, but the main purpose and hope of this legislation is to make it more difficult for trouble-minded young men — who have disobeyed no law until they feel impelled to kill innocent people — to acquire clips with many rounds, thus reducing the number of children murdered.

Unfortunately, we cannot believe that no such person can ever acquire large clips, but if in another slaughter just one child is saved because the killer has run out of ammunition, then the limitation is well worth enacting. If the writer doubts this, let him speak with one of the parents who have lost a child.

Richard Lettis

(I should have added that few criminals use one hundred bullets
to commit their crimes, and that, in any case, it is not they who are
slaughtering our children but mentally disturbed young men who now can
get all the ammunition they may want.)

2014, August 10th, The Record

From: *The Record*, August 4:

Lawsuit against Obama is justified

The argument:

Commenting on the question of whether Republicans will attempt to impeach President Obama, the letter argues that "It is, in fact, the Democrats who are raising the specter of impeachment in hopes of turning the midterm election focus away from the plethora of administration scandals, not Republicans or Tea Party spokespeople." He offers several "reasons why those who oppose Obama do not favor impeachment," to wit:

* If convicted, the succession would fall to Vice President Joseph Biden, who many feel has long since demonstrated his unfitness for the office.

* By the time the impeachment process was completed, Obama's term will be effectively over in any case.

* Republicans and Tea Party members believe in our constitutional form of government. A third impeachment exercise in 40 years would threaten the fabric of our form of government and turn this last-resort mechanism into the sort of "no confidence" procedure that in parliamentary forms of democracy brings down the elected leadership without the expressed direction of the electorate."

From: *The Record*, August 10:

The reply:

I think I need some help in understanding this letter (August 4). Though its title claims the lawsuit is justified, the writer immediately argues that it is "the Democrats who are raising the specter of impeachment." So the Republicans are threatening

183

impeachment, but it is the Democrats who are really interested in it, because they want to turn "the midterm election focus away from the plethora of administration scandals." (Do I have it so far?)

The reason the anti-Obama faction does not want what it is trying to do is that if President Obama got kicked out, Vice President Joe Biden would take over, and he has "long since demonstrated his unfitness for the office," according to the letter. So the Republicans would, I guess, go through with the impeachment if Biden would make a good Democratic president? And by the time Obama got himself impeached, he'd be out of office. Still, as the letter's title says, the lawsuit is justified? Let's go ahead and do what we don't want to do?

But I wish the writer had given us more about the plethora of scandals he attributes to the Obama administration (and also list a few of the awful things that Biden has done). I do recall some difficulties the administration has gotten itself into, but I'll be darned if I understood they were a truckload or so. In any case, the writer speaks not of mistakes, nor blamable action, nor even regrettable political doings, but of "scandals." That is, they, all of them, deeply offend our sense of decency, just like, say, when Vice President Dick Cheney decided, against the law of his country, that we should water board (nearly drown) some of our prisoners, over and over.

Well, the writer will have to refresh my memory. I just don't remember a ton or so of this kind of thing from Obama.

Richard Lettis

(The issue here was whether the Republicans should try to prove illegal acts by the president. But the question of whether this would benefit or would hurt their reputation became a serious problem, and the attempt was dropped. No doubt there was more to this tempest than I (or the writer) am aware of.)

2014, September 17th, The Record

From: *The Record*, September 13:

Don't pick and choose God's rules

The argument:

The writer finds it interesting that the Editorial Page Editor's
focus as he writes about the Deity and his commandments is limited to
certain sins in church teachings." The Editor finds poverty, violence,
and social injustice to be bad but says that sexual deviation is good.
The writer then shifts to God's mercy for sinners (the assumption
seeming to be that gay sex is *not* good, but if the Bible is indeed
God's word, complete and error-free, "then it communicates God's
wonderful mercy to those who ask for it. And judgment to those who do
not believe they deserve it." He then asks how we can tell "what God
is serious about and what he is only kidding about," and so "It is a
huge gamble to presume on God's accuracy." And he concludes with a
comparison to help us understand: "As a rainbow is complete with all
its colors, so God is complete with all his good rules." (As the
reader may see, this is a difficult letter to summarize and make
sense.)

From: *The Record*, September 17:

Regarding "Don't pick and choose God's rules" (September 13):

The reply:

If the writer holds the Bible as God's word, he may want to
rethink his advice against looking over and carefully selecting among
the rules of The Intelligent Designer. Though most of them are highly
commendable, there are a few one may wish to forget seeing. I would
hesitate, for example, whether I really want to obey the rule about
how to treat my slaves, or the one that insist that I kill my children
if they are disrespectful. And I think I'll not go out and slay non-

believers, though several injunctions tell me I have to.

Even the commandment of Jesus (who is not so much a lawman as his Old Testament Dad) has at least one objectionable rule, that which commanded his disciples to "hate" their families if they wanted to follow him. (I am not clear whether this applies to all followers, or just the disciples; which, if it's the former, could use some explanation.) This rainbow of Biblical recording of Divine commands, to which the writer refers, has a few unpleasant shades that mar the whole.

Richard Lettis

2014, Sept/Oct, The Yale Alumni Magazine

From: *The Yale Alumni Magazine*, June/July, 2014:
Who was first? Who cares?

The argument:
The cover story for the May/June issue, "Who Was the First
African American Student at Yale?" was, a letter subsequently charged,
"an embarrassment." "It is well known," the letter said, "that Yale
has a history of discrimination against blacks and Jews in the
admissions process. It now appears that Yale is going out of its way
to demonstrate just how many blacks and Jews actually were admitted,"
and went on to delineate several ways in which the identification of a
student as black was of no value.

(The editors pointed out several things that answered the
numerous criticisms, for example that the University of Yale could not
be held responsible for what its alumnus magazine did, since it had no
control over the publication.)

Two other letters offered what must be considered rantings,
charging Yale with various faults, one saying that the article was a
waste of time: "What do we really want to commemorate? That some
people are darker than others, that some people can be black and
Jewish, that people's complexions differ, that some people ignore
color and others don't? Do we really need a hundred years of scholarly
research and verbiage to arrive at these astounding conclusions? "That
some writers wish to expend time and money on this nonsense is not a
reason for others to find it worthy of publication," and at long last
finished with "It behooves me to reluctantly say that it sounds as
though the writers must be sorry to read an authentic experience
attesting to the innate fairness of American people, so eager are they

to characterize us negatively." And a third letter declared that "Your obsession with race is unbecoming, absurd, endlessly tiresome, and-- strange to say--racist. With this article you are in effect saying, "Wow, a black guy was smart enough to get into Yale in 1857." My answer is, "Who cares?" I felt that the writers of these angry commentators was a case of hyper-PC, the nervous assumption that anything that mentions race is going to be prejudiced, and so I responded.)

From: the *Yale Alumni Magazine*, Sept/Oct. 2014:
The reply:

In response to the outraged--and not far from outrageous--letters protesting your interest in and articles about Yale's first African- American graduate, I would say that to mention race is not to be bigoted. To insist that racism's role in our country's history must be ignored is to ignore Faulkner's well-known comment that the past is "not even past."

Awareness of what we have been is essential to our becoming something better. And the magazine's interest in Yale's first black student is not, as one letter-writer had it, equivalent to saying "Wow, a black guy was smart enough to get into Yale," but rather to record one of the innumerable steps we have taken toward racial equality.

Richard Lettis

(I was reminded of an incident I witnessed while a member of a church which had gathered together with other churches to consider ways of helping combat racism. Among the several suggestions was one a representative offered, "We have the best solution at our church, we just all agree not to talk about it." The rest of us exchanged glances, knowing that silence can be the ally of bigotry. Jarod Kintz said that "Ignoring a problem is the same as being ignorant of it.")

2014, October 17th, The Record

From: *The Record*, October 17:

Euthanasia not compassionate.

The argument:

The writer accuses an unnamed organization of being "intent on convincing the public that assisted suicide and euthanasia are compassionate and merciful. They are biased against life-sustaining measures and biased for imposed death." She speaks of a case in which, she says, a patient (quoting a previous letter) "suffered unnecessarily," "suffered in agony for days" and had a "horrendous experience." What, she asked, "caused the suffering, agony and horror? Food and water. But when these two forms of torture were withdrawn, [the patient] died "mercifully." Her comment: "I fail to see how withdrawing food and water improves care at any point in life." She asks, "As for choice, are they in favor of a choice that treats food and water as ordinary care, because of the dignity of the patient as a human being?" And she answers: "No." And she concludes: "Would they defend my choice to receive life-sustaining treatment if it were ignored and death were imposed against my wishes? I doubt it. Whenever you hear the word 'choice' used where human life is concerned, think very carefully about what this choice really offers."

From: *The Record*, October 17, 2014:

Regarding "Euthanasia not compassionate" (Your Views, Oct. 17, 2014):

The reply:

The illogic of the letter is not easy to unscramble. After quoting the description of a person who "suffered in agony," the writer asks "what caused the suffering, agony and horror? Food and water." And then says, "I fail to see how withdrawing food and water

189

improves care."

The writer seems not to understand what euthanasia means: the withholding of food and water are not as she said "two forms of torture," but the means by which the torture from some other source is ended; they are withdrawn so the sufferer may mercifully die rather than live in agony.

The next paragraph is almost completely beyond understanding: "As for choice, are they in favor of a choice that treats food and water as ordinary care, because of the dignity of the patient as human being? No."

All I can make of this is the writer simply does not understand that it is by no means an "ordinary" situation but rather an extreme one in which the sufferer decides to end a life that holds nothing except unendurable pain; his or her "dignity" is in no way involved, except perhaps the dignity of one courageous enough to end life rather than endure.

The most we can make of all this is that the writer seems to believe that some group akin to Sarah Palin's fictional "death panel" decides to kill off a sufferer even though he or she does not want to die, which is of course totally against the idea of euthanasia. It is the dying person who has chosen, and anything else is still called murder and is against the law.

(To clarify: the writer was responding to a case in which a person who had decided to die was not given food. This was done, of course, not to give torture but to end it.)

Richard Lettis

From: *The Record*, December 1:

Regarding "Christie's campaign not like Obama's" (Your Views, Nov. 27):

The argument:

Commenting on a previous letter, the writer of this charges that

"The writer's recitation of the 'facts' ignores certain realities." He cannot understand how it can be said that "Obamacare is working as promised," when "Dr. Jonathan Gruber's comments have come to light and when we know that the administration's promise of 'If you like your doctor, you can keep your doctor. If you like your plan, you can keep your plan' is false." He also calls the stated unemployment rate inaccurate, declaring that "in October 2014, the real unemployment rate was 11.5 percent, nearly double the official rate of 5.8 percent, which does not take into account the number of Americans who are underemployed or who have simply stopped seeking unemployment benefits." As for President Obama's taking troops out of Iraq, that was a "premature action, against the advice of his military commanders," which "led to the rise of ISIS for which Obama admitted he had no plan for dealing with." Still another accusation is the fact that our national debt has soared from $10 trillion to almost $18 trillion today. No wonder that Democrats ran away from Obama in the midterm elections.

2014, December 5th, The Record

From: *The Record*, December 5, 2014:

The reply:

Here are the charges leveled in the letter (December1) against President Obama:

1. He promised one could keep his doctor and plan under Obamacare. This has not been done, so the current statement that it is working "as promised" is false.

This confuses two different promises, the first made in Obama's campaign, and the second mentioning the fact that now the Health Care Act is performing its task. And Obama was not lying in his first promise. He was prevented from keeping it because of the massive changes he had to concede before the bill could be passed.

2. "The real unemployment rate was 11.5 percent, nearly double the official rate of 5.8 percent."

The insinuation is that the government is lying, but all statistics for past years have been figured in the current manner, which is not to include certain groups such as those who have ceased to seek employment, so that if these were added, every figure recorded for past presidents would be increased in the same way.

3. Obama's pulling troops out of Iraq has led to the rise of ISIS.

If this act was indeed a fault, it was committed under massive national pressure, and with the laudable desire to save the lives of young Americans.

4. Obama is to blame for the fact that "our national debt has soared from $10 trillion to almost $18 trillion."

But that increase, in a time of unstable economy, seems not so bad when compared with President Bush's $5.849 trillion with a

steadier economy; it more than doubled the national debt. Obama went
into debt to save the economy; why did G. W. Bush?

Republicans are good at things like this, giving a slant to
information, melodramatic enough to make newspaper headlines, while
the difficult and less exciting refutation of the charge is given
little notice.

(The following report somewhat reduces the previous writer's
delight in Dr. Gruber's comments:

Jonathan Gruber, the health economist whose incendiary comments
about "the stupidity of the American voter" have embarrassed the Obama
administration, apologized on Tuesday for what he described as his
"glib, thoughtless and sometimes downright insulting comments."

"I am not a political adviser nor a politician," said Dr. Gruber,
a professor at the Massachusetts Institute of Technology who was a
paid consultant to the Obama administration in 2009 to 2010.

Dr. Gruber minimized his role, saying he had used an "economic
microsimulation model" to help the administration and Democrats in
Congress assess the impact of policies in the Affordable Care Act. He
later defended the law in a number of speeches. In one, he said the
law had been adopted, in part, because of the stupidity of voters and
a "lack of transparency" about its financing.

Testifying on Tuesday before the House Committee on Oversight and
Government Reform, Dr. Gruber said: "I behaved badly, and I will have
to live with that, but my own inexcusable arrogance is not a flaw in
the Affordable Care Act. The A.C.A. is a milestone accomplishment for
our nation that already has provided millions of Americans with health
insurance."

The chairman of the committee, Representative Darrell Issa,
Republican of California, said backers of the law had passed it and
sold it to the public with half-truths and deception. He added that
Dr. Gruber and the administration had displayed "a pattern of
intentionally misleading the public about the true nature and impact

of Obamacare."

The senior Democrat on the committee, Representative Elijah E. Cummings of Maryland, joined in the criticism of Dr. Gruber. He said his comments were "absolutely stupid" and "incredibly disrespectful." Worse, he said, the statements gave Republicans "a political gift in their relentless campaign to tear down" the law.

Mr. Issa showed a video in which Dr. Gruber suggests that supporters of the health law had written it in such a way that the Congressional Budget Office would not count required premium payments as tax revenue.

"This bill was written in a tortured way to make sure C.B.O. did not score the mandate as taxes," Dr. Gruber says in the October 2013 video. "Lack of transparency is a huge political advantage. And basically, call it the 'stupidity of the American voter' or whatever, but basically that was really, really critical to getting the thing to pass."

He appeared to squirm on Tuesday under questioning by Republicans who confronted him with his own past statements. He did not deny or recant those statements, but said he regretted some of his impolitic formulations. "I made a series of statements that were really just inexcusable," Dr. Gruber said toward the end of the four-hour hearing.

"It is never appropriate to try to make oneself seem more important or smarter by demeaning others," he also said. "I know better. I knew better. I am embarrassed, and I am sorry."

Dr. Gruber infuriated Republicans on the committee by refusing to disclose the total amount of money he had received in grants and contracts from the federal government and states for work related to the Affordable Care Act. He also declined to say if he would provide copies of documents that he had prepared for federal and state agencies.

Representative Jason Chaffetz, Republican of Utah, told Dr. Gruber: "You have been paid by the American taxpayers. Will you provide that information to this committee?"

Dr. Gruber replied repeatedly, "You can take it up with my counsel."

In an interview, Mr. Chaffetz said he would insist on the requests after he becomes the panel's chairman in January. "Mr. Gruber will cough up those documents one way or another," he said.

Though he strongly supports the health law, Dr. Gruber has made statements that appear to undercut arguments now being pushed by the Obama administration in court cases challenging the payment of premium subsidies in states using the federal insurance exchange. Under the law, the federal government provides a backstop if states fail to establish exchanges.

"What's important to remember politically about this is if you're a state and you don't set up an exchange, that means your citizens don't get their tax credits," Dr. Gruber said in 2012.

By contrast, the White House has said that Congress intended for the subsidies to be available nationwide, in all states, regardless of whether they had a federal or state-run exchange.

Dr. Gruber said his earlier comments had been referring to the possibility that the federal government might not create a federal exchange.

"Your new explanation of your previous public statements makes little sense," Representative Justin Amash, Republican of Michigan, told him.

(A version of this article appears in print on December 10, 2014, on page A22 of the New York edition with the headline: "Economist Says He's Sorry for 'Arrogance' on Health Law.")

Richard Lettis, Ph.D

2014, January 14th, The Record

From: *The Record*, January 14:

Pope Francis is to the Vatican as President Obama is to Washington, D.C.

The argument:

Despite the fact that President Obama and the Pope are of different ethnic and religious backgrounds, this letter finds "similarities are remarkable." Obama, he says, "is a progressive who violates the Constitution and has obstructed Congress with the help of former Senate Majority Leader Harry Reid. He supports combating global warming, has divided the country, has a disdain for capitalism and is in bed politically with Fidel Castro." The writer seems to have added several items which are not clearly relevant to his argument, but now he says that "Likewise, Pope Francis is a progressive liberal, who is attempting to change Canon Law (equivalent to our Constitution), which prohibits divorced and remarried Catholics from receiving Communion." The Pope inhibits conservative bishops and supports global warming, has "divided the Catholic Church by publicly demeaning the conservatives," has also supported the U.S. policy changes regarding Cuba, and "clearly states that he is in favor of socialism over trickle-down economics." Personally, the write is grateful for Ronald Reagan and Pope John Paul II, "who through capitalism defeated the Soviet Union. He takes comfort in the fact that Obama will be gone in two years, and hopes Pope Francis will resign, before he can do more harm to the church. "As a practicing Catholic," he concludes, "I will not be surprised if there is a schism within the Catholic Church during Francis' reign."

2015, January, The Record

From: *The Record,* January:

The reply:

In the natural course of things, Democrats frequently disagree with Republican convictions, but usually they do not accuse. The Republicans, on the other hand, frequently find the Democrats to be morally wrong in their beliefs. The January 14 letter, for example, says that President Obama "violates the Constitution," by which the writer really means Obama has done some things he does not like, but chooses a moral word to express it. Obama has done nothing that other presidents have done, and would not have to do anything if Republicans had helped pass acts which in the past they have approved.

Republicans also frequently shift blame for troubles from themselves to their political opponents; thus it is not they who have "obstructed Congress," but the Democrats, a charge that is ludicrous when one examines the evidence and finds that, as said, Republicans have voted against almost anything the president has proposed.

The writer also uses loaded words in his disagreements. Obama has not merely done some questionable things about capitalism, but has shown "a disdain" for it. The writer has a right to object to the government's easing of relations with Cuba, but he again reveals his use of excess when he says that the president "is in bed politically with Fidel Castro." The simple truth about reason is that it almost always ceases to function when emotion arises.

It is no surprise to find that the writer also dislikes Pope Francis. He may well be right about "a schism within the Catholic Church." The bitter truth, I suggest, is that a schism is, like many unhappy things, an unfortunate necessity. The Pope sees that in the last few decades his church has weakened, and he seeks to save it by bringing it closer to our contemporary world, while conservatives fight to maintain the old ways.

Richard Lettis

(It is Church Dictum that the Pope is never wrong, but more than a few conservative church voices say that in this matter he is. Each Catholic must make a decision: to support the Pope or those who attack him. The most likely result of this is a division in Catholicism. This may not be bad: Catholicism is on its way downward, and needs to do something to halt the slide.)

2015, Febraury 15th, The Record

From: *The Record*, February 8:

The President's misguided policies

The argument:

The writer argues that President Obama's statement that "the overwhelming majority of Muslims reject radical Islam and "the medieval interpretation of Islam is rejected by 99.9 percent of Muslims" is a platitude he has beaten to death, leaving wondering "where exactly are we on all of this?" He calls out attention to "demonstrations attended by millions of people rallying from Paris to Tokyo, calling for an end to radical Islam," while "many Muslim rallies and demonstrations have been directed at the destruction of the Western world in general, and the Christian and Jewish populations in particular." If "even . . . a very small number of the 99.9 percent of Muslims who allegedly reject radical Islamic terrorism took a stand for humanity, you would have millions of voices denouncing what is supposedly believed by only a tiny fraction of Muslims, making the Paris and Tokyo demonstrations pale in comparison. Obama's immediate concern seems to be "more about burnishing the image of the Muslim world, and not in combating radical Islamic terrorism."

From: *The Record*, February 15:

The Reply:

I have neither the knowledge nor the ability to judge, as does the writer of "The president's misguided policies" (February 8, 2015), how many Muslims desire "the destruction of the Western world in general, and the Christian and Jewish population in particular." I can only suggest that the past shows how disastrous it can be to condemn a large group of people (Negroes are lazy and oversexed, Jews are stingy and liable to cheat you, women are weak and over-emotional and not too bright). But I can take issue with the objectionable devices he uses to criticize President Obama.

The president's statement that "the medieval interpretation of Islam is rejected by 99.9 percent of Muslims" is a "platitude" which has been "beaten to death," an obvious use of degrading hyperbole (it takes a while to create a platitude, and much longer to kill it) which is constantly used by conservative critics. And the charge that "Obama's immediate concern is more about burnishing the image of the Muslim world, and not combatting Islamic terror, is but one more case of conservative pretense to discern a motive without justification.

Why would our president want to make Islam seem better than it is; what fell object could he have in mind? Have we not learned that it is wiser and more successful to try to deal with threatening countries than to go to war with them--have we learned nothing from Iraq and Afghanistan? And does it not say something about the president that he is joining in the effort to subdue the worst of the Muslim world in his sending armed forces to combat them?

But no; Obama can do no right. We need no evidence to find in him a base and evil motive for every action, each of which is dastardly wrong and illogical. Let's bring back George Bush, who we know did so many things right, and never got us in trouble.

Richard Lettis

2015, March 4th, The Record

From: *The Record*, March 4:

Regarding "Email issue revives Clinton concerns"

The argument:

Why, the letter asks, "does Hillary Clinton, on the eve of her becoming secretary of state, secretly set up her own private email system that is administered by unknown parties and that provides an unknown level of security against cyber-attacks, and commence to use this system for all of her official email . . . during her four years in office?" "More importantly," he adds, "this rogue email operation must have been discovered early on by Homeland Security and made known to the White House. If so, why would the White House tolerate such an egregious breach of protocol, let alone common sense?" All this calls "into serious question not only Clinton's judgment and management skills, but also, and more importantly, her basic ethics and ability to follow standard government protocols. A person of such profile has no business seeking the presidency."

From: *The Record*, March:

Regarding "Clinton's judgment not presidential" (March 4):

The reply:

I agree with the writer's concern about Clinton's misuse of email until I come to his question: "What was the motivation?" The writer never answers this query, but clearly the implication is that Clinton's reason for a "secretly set up . . . private email system" is done for some unacceptable purpose. She has created a "rogue email operation," an "egregious breach of protocol." Surely the question asked must be answered before such accusing expressions are used. Certainly Ms. Clinton has violated protocol, but the writer knows no more than I why she did so. For evil proposes? For doing things that are objectionable? Perhaps, but if we accept the trial court's "innocent until proven guilty," we should wait until there is evidence for any conclusion. And the writer's dragging "the White House" into the situation, which must have ""known" about her impropriety, raises the suspicion that this letter is not so much an objective and impartial criticism of Clinton as one more hyperbolic attempt to discredit the Administration.

This possibility is quickly confirmed by what follows: the misuse of email systems calls "into serious question not only Clinton's judgment . . . but also . . . her . . . ability to follow standard government protocols." And (and here is the *writer's* "motivation") "A person of such profile has no business seeking the presidency." All this, then, has been but one more effort to twist anything into a reason to vote Republican.

I wonder: did the writer declare that Governor Christie's GWB scandal (either he knew about it--which, given his acerbic personality, seems likely-- or should have known) make him unfit for the highest office? Jeb Bush governs a state that allows a person to kill anyone if he claimed he felt threatened, and Bush continues to admit his charter school program has failed--enough, surely to rule him out too?

And finally, is it not true that we hope to find in a good president high intelligence, considerable experience, and full commitment, all of which Clinton has? To rule her out for one mistake is like firing a very good waitress because, on one occasion, she sneaked a cookie out of a jar.

Richard Lettis

2015, April 29th, The Record

From: *The Record*, April:

The argument:

The writer is "a modern Orthodox Jew," a sect which feels "fully comfortable shaking hands with women or sitting next to them." But recently, when he offered his hand to a Muslim woman, he found that she "politely declined my handshake." "I withdrew my hand in understanding and respect for her cultural and religious beliefs," he writes, explaining that "In a society such as ours, where freedom to peacefully one's religious beliefs is a cornerstone of our history, we should all recognize and appreciate the important difference between a privately held opinion and adherence to one's religious laws."

From: *The Record*, April 29:

Regarding "Religious views deserve respect":

The reply:

Though one must respect this well written and compassionate letter, it is unfortunately necessary to disagree with what it says. The writer recounts an incident in which a Muslim woman politely declined to shake his hand. He was not offended, for he understood that "her cultural and religious beliefs" required her to decline to shake the hand of a man.

The writer was following an age old custom of accepting a religious dictum without question. But this kind of blind obedience has in good part changed; today we have, more and more frequently, when subject to a religious law, decided that we would not accept it unless it was made clear that there was good reason for the commandment. In doing so, we have added religious views to the same kind of examination that is required for all laws and commandments. For example:

> **Question:** why must I always drive on the right side of the road?
> **Answer:** free choice would in this case lead to innumerable disasters.
> **Question:** why must I pay taxes?
> **Answer:** because without it you would have no government.
> **Question:** why can't I sit in my backyard and play loud music at 3 A. M.?
> **Answer:** your neighbors need some sleep.
> **Question:** why should a Muslim woman refuse to shake a man's hand?
> **Answer:**

No longer can modern society permit religion to make commandments without a why, for to do so may encourage acts which are harmful to some or all members of society. I am not acquainted with Muslim law, but the commandment in question would seem to be prejudicial to women, a companion to religious regulations which have forbidden a woman to be alone in a room with a man, or drive a car, or bare her head. Religious views do indeed deserve respect, but they also must, like any other commandment, explain their intention, so that they may be assessed.

Richard Lettis

(On the day after this letter was published, an answering letter appeared, a surprising speed in comparison with the usual practice of several days between first letter and answering letter. I was accused of making "the case that . . . there is no justification for obeying religious laws, which, to him, are just blindly followed with no reason." To refute this charge of mine, she offers a reason for the refused handshake that started all this: "In order to protect and secure the sacred bonds of husband and wife, which ultimately protect the family unit, Orthodox Jews do not shake hands with the opposite sex." She leaves it to us to understand how a handshake can endanger a married couple and its family, but the answer seems obvious: physical contact between sexes can lead to, well, you know, the naughty stuff. Thus far do the Muslim and Orthodox religions take the prim and puritanical idea that sex lurks everywhere, ready to rear its wicked head at the first (and least) opportunity. I have shaken the hands of a fair number of women--some of them rather attractive--without, as far as I know, engendering shameful and family-threatening heat (though, on looking back, I wish it sometimes had). There is an offensive distrust of us all in this thinking, a conviction that we may, upon the slightest opportunity, heave ourselves into erotic fury, thereby wrecking marriages and condemning the little ones to a one-parent childhood. Still, I am grateful to the lady's letter, for it adds an important step to the process I presented in my letter. I merely said that every commandment--anywhere, not just religion, Madam--should be justified by offering a reason for the rule. But there needs be one more step: the reason must stand examination, and if it is as gosh-darn silly as finding corrupting cohabitation in the touch of two hands, the commandment must be consigned to the utter-nonsense paper shredder. We scandalous moderns sometimes even go so far as to exchange a greeting kiss (and hug!) between the sexes without winding up in divorce court.)

2015, May 24th, The Record

(In May 1215, the Governor of Florida, Jeb Bush, was queried about evidence to support the rights of gays. As cited below, he replied that he saw nothing in the Constitution that did.)

From: *The Record*, May 24:

Comment:

How should we respond to Gov. Bush's recent comment on the Constitution? He said that he sees nothing in the document concerning the rights of gay people, and no doubt he is right. But is it the implication of his statement that therefore gays have no rights? If so, several serious questions must be answered: since the rights of the black race are also not mentioned, did we err in freeing them from slavery and granting them the rights of all other citizens? I do not believe that women are afforded any rights in the Constitution; shall we take away their right to vote? The governor's comment raises these and several other vital concerns; one must hope that he will provide us with answers anon.

The real question, of course, is whether we should, like Justice Scalia, settle all questions by reference to the Constitution as it stands, or accept the argument that time has raised problems which the Constitution did not anticipate, and therefore we must act according to the best resolution of difficulties we can realize. Indeed, it seems reasonable that some changes and additions to the Constitution are necessary.

Time inevitably produces change; the rules and convictions of any document must be found insufficient for the needs of later years — even the Bible, arguably the greatest source to which we may turn in time of trouble, now contains commandments which we no longer can accept (approval of slavery, the inferiority of women, the destruction of all those of another faith). How could our founding fathers anticipate the problem of fracking, the moral question of drones, the difficulties of immigration? This was well understood by perhaps the greatest of these men, Thomas Jefferson, participator in the writing of the writer of the Constitution and author of the Declaration of Independence, who said that he expected the document to require considerable changes and additions in the future. It may well be agreed that we no longer have the leaders of his stature, but we must be content to work with what and whom we have, strong enough to modify and develop, realizing that some of these changes may have been wrong and willing to replace them as may be necessary. We see today to have lost much of the courage and energy with which our nation began; it is time to regain these qualities.

Richard Lettis

2015, August 8th, The Record

From: *The Record,* June 19:

Argument:

Everything is so bad--morality, economy, credibility--that we should take a chance on Donald Trump, who is a businessman, loves his country, and is worth a try

From: *The Record,* June 23:

The reply:

I thought I had seen the most inept letter to be printed in The Record, but the writer of "Trump's worth a try" has proved me wrong. He need not have begun by saying he has had not much political opinion, for the letter, which drips with misstatement and unfounded assumptions, makes the point by itself. He claims a "downward spiral of morals" (yes, like our finally giving those of a different sexual orientation the right to full citizenship), likewise of the economy (now doing so well the Republicans are reduced to pea-shooter criticism or to ignoring the subject entirely), and of "credibility" (he presumably means by the Tea Party, which would not believe Obama if he said the earth is round).

Trump may (given the chance) fix all this because he is a businessman, though that occupation is not now generally known to produce great presidents. And things are now so desperate that Trump's "worth a try" is surely the lowest and most pessimistic idea extant, suggesting that for the leadership of our country we can do no more than toss the dice and hope. "What have we got to lose?" he concludes.

Well, our country, surely, our country.

From: *The Record*, August 5:

Argument:

In "Accountability goes both ways," the question of whether body cameras for the police are useful. He begins by defending the police, attributing the "bad things" (i.e. the killing of black men) to their "being human" and having to make "split-decisions." The same people who spoke against traffic light cameras now are for body cameras, suggesting the camera "is just to be used only when it works in favor of one's agenda."

From: *The Record*, August 8:

The reply:

I much appreciate the writer of "Accountability goes both ways" for getting some complicated things straight. You see, the reason some bad things have happened (like the several unarmed black men who have been shot down) is simply that the cops are human, and have to make split decisions (e.g., "shall I kill this unarmed man or not?"). There's a fairly good chance that the police are right more often than not, so let's not get fired up about the few slips when helpless people die (we should just say "oops"). The idea of having body cameras which could show what the policeman is doing is questionable, because they are "not a panacea for our policing problems, but merely for enhancing police accountability"--and do we really need that? What's really needed is *public* accountability: those who disliked traffic light cameras are the same who are now demanding police cameras, which means they just want a camera "when it works in favor of one's agenda" (like getting evidence when a bad cop murders somebody). After all, running a red light is a bad thing too (though perhaps not as bad as young black men lying dead on our streets).

Well, glad all that got cleared up. Now how about serial killers?

Richard Lettis

2015, August 30th, The Record

From: *The Record*, August 26:

The argument:

The presidential candidates are criticized for "allowing the fourteenth amendment to stand," because it will continue to "let lawbreakers enter our borders to have their babies." We will pay the medical expenses, and do nothing about those who are breaking the law by entering, but the politicians seem to accept this, since "no legislative action has been taken to counteract this very serious problem." The fourteenth amendment was passed to grant citizenship to slaves and their children, not those who enter our Country without permission to have children here. The writer recommends the creation of a third party called "the Common Sense Party," and says he will vote for its candidate, no matter who he is.

From: *The Record*, August 30:

The reply:

Among all the ranting and heat of the debate about immigrants, there is one word that is sorely needed but hardly ever used. The word is "compassion."

Certainly the recent "GOP caving on citizenship" does not mention the word or what it means: it criticizes immigrants for crossing our borders "to have their babies," but gives no thought to those simply looking for jobs, or escape from troubled areas, or the chance to rise to the poverty line or at last feed their children.

Richard Lettis, Ph.D

Let us consider those babies--what should we feel about them? The writer is concerned only with the fact that we may have to pay the doctors' bills, which seems a somewhat cold-blooded way to think about children; I suggest we may do better to think of pitiable infants whose parents seek only to be able to give them food and provide a decent shelter.

I wonder what those who agree with this writer would do if they found themselves on the wrong side of a border, their side with starving children while on the other side there are healthy babies. Illegal, of course, to cross. Ah, I assume they would insist on staying where they are; good people don't break laws, not even for ailing infants.

But some may argue that there is something more important even than laws, as some of our ancestors (Thoreau, for example) knew when they refused to pay taxes to a government that tolerated bigotry. Those babies crossing the border are human, and humanity must precede borders and money-counting complainers. Either we ought to follow the dictum on the Statue of Liberty, or we ought to tear it down.

Richard Lettis

2015, Sept/Oct, The Yale Alumni Magazine

From: The Yale Alumni Magazine, September-October:

It is regrettable that the last issue of a publication associated with a great university stooped to the use of a euphemism. To say that Mr. Charles Townsend "passed away" is to diminish the hard fact that he died, deprived of the stern reality of one of the two most important parts of our lives. "Passed away" suggests a rather cozy removal from here to some place else; if this makes it easier for us to take, it also makes it harder to grasp the full force of his ceasing to be.

It would seem that the future may call us the age of euphemism, taking the edge off anything that doesn't sound nice: there are no more "used" cars, but plenty of "pre-owned" ones, and "armpits" have disappeared in favor of "underarms." And we will be known as the people who lacked the strength to recognize and endure what is, preferring our little not too bad.

If you should chance to record my death, kindly let it be what it is: I will be nowhere else, I will be nowhere, and I'd like people to feel all that that means.

Richard Lettis '57

Richard Lettis, Ph.D

2015, October 14th, The Record

From: *The Record,* October 8:

The argument:

The Record reported that the evangelist Billy Graham had written in his latest book that all non-Christians would go to hell.

From: *The Record,* October 14:

The reply:

To comment on Billy Graham's recent dictum that all non-Christians are headed for hell, one must walk a couple of miles, heave stones at anything (preferably not a policeman), run through one's list of naughty words, take a deep breath, remember what Christ said on the cross and start the computer.

Is this what good Christians do?

Those who do not enlist in "Grahamania" do not give him much thought. He is just a kindly old man who has been may be more or less good for some people. But as Willy Loman's wife said, now attention must be paid, if we find that there is an influential man who happily condemns the great majority of mankind to eternal suffering. We must not let the horror of the phrase slipped by: have you ever had a second-degree burn? How long did it hurt?

Second, one is struck by the pure heartlessness of the

declaration. Calmly and easily condemns the majority of human beings. We can only hope he hasn't thought or felt the real meaning of what he says. If a plague threatened to wipe out four-fifths of mankind, would he really accept it calmly?

But the most important thing, surely, is how Christianity takes this madness; anything other than rejection merits the utmost condemnation of this already damaged faith.

Richard Lettis

2015, March 10th, Additional Entry

(As my reader may have guessed from the number of letters published in the Bergen *Record*, it is my local paper. *The Record* accepts just one letter per month, which makes sense but has not infrequently left me in high frustration as I read something that cried out for an answer (sometimes too, I grudgingly admit, the letter was simply not accepted). I provide a few example below.)

From: *The Record*, March 3:

The argument:

The writer expressed her objection to the swimsuit issue of Sports Illustrated, declaring that some of the photos of scarcely clad models "could have a negative and demeaning impact." But still worse, she added, is the "constant barrage of erectile dysfunction commercials on television, one of which, she said "bordered on porn."

Additional Entry: March 10:

The reply:

When I see such a letter as the above, I get the heebeejeebees, The writer herself admits that revealing pictures of models only "could have" a negative impact, but that mere possibility is enough to prompt her to take the time to write a letter. She does not take the time to suggest what the impact could be--male readers will go out and rape women? Women with less attractive figures will commit suicide?

But wait: it gets worse. There is indeed a problem with the erectile dysfunction commercials, but it is the reverse of her idea. I don't think I have ever seen anything so devoid of sex (and here the subject is sex!): we see a couple walk on the beach, another papering a wall, a third sitting at a restaurant table. And that's all. Granted, in a couple of scenes we see them holding hands, but I have never considered this as "bordering on pornography."

That we have yet to learn to react normally to sex is clear from such a complaint. The human body is *not* indecent, obscene, or fatal to human society. How much longer will it take to accept that we are just animals, who cover ourselves for warmth, or attractiveness, or to conceal less than stunning figures, but *not* for "decency"?

Richard Lettis

From my head, March:

Comment:
From: *The Record,* June:

Argument: See answering letter..

Additiona Entry: June:

The reply:

Memorial

The recent Memorial Day brought forth a letter in which the writer suggested that "We should also have remembered those who fought against us." This predictably brought forth another letter angrily

217

denouncing the "evil" idea. The suggestion was not only wrong but dangerous, a "foolish idea" diverting our attention from the brave men of our own armed forces to think of "the people who kill them." The two letters raise an issue of great importance: should we think of ourselves as the good guys and all who warred against us as the bad guys, or should we regard them simply as young men who fought for their countries as ours did for our country, and find it in us to forgive and to think of them as worthy of our compassion?

When stripped of its hyperbole, the second letter is difficult to argue against: many of the countries which fought us were governed by evil minded men who, had they triumphed, would have brought disaster upon us all. The battle in which we are now engaged is a powerful example, its leaders perpetrating atrocities and threatening to force their ideology upon other countries. But are we sure we can blame their soldiers for obeying these leaders and waging a war, however terribly wrong? When this war is over, is it conceivable that our soldiers might forgive those soldiers and even engage in meeting them and discussing the war?

An answer may be found in another war, one as fierce, as disastrous, as those of the present conflict. But some time ago American soldiers initiated contact with Japanese soldiers: they met and talked and discussed their own parts in the battles, and they found that they could respect and associate with each other — nothing evil or dangerous or wrong resulting. They were not concerned with which side was right, which governments were condemnable; they were simply men who had gone through a terrible experience and now realized that it was something they had shared, had had in common. (One may add to this a single soldier, the hero of Laura Hildebrand's "Unbroken," who looked up the guards in his concentration camp and forgave them all.)

For too long we wretched humans have thrived upon hatred of anything that is different from us: the color of skin, the sex, the nationality, the contrary idea, the different religion. It may be said that these compassionate soldiers, and the writer of the first letter, have decided that the "we" are the good guys and "they" are the bad ones kind of thinking has led us into far more danger and destruction than anything the second letter could imagine. We may find in history the gradual replacing of "we" and "they" with "us," struggling to leave behind fear and hatred, to be replaced with compassion and understanding. There is a French saying that is relevant: "tout comprendre c'est tout pardonner" — to know all is to forgive all. I think that one of the greatest men in our history would have liked that; his name was Jesus.

Richard Lettis

We poor mortals are encased in a body that will sooner or later extrude us, either into a world to come or into nothing, so I suppose it is understandable that our vulnerable container alarms us and we insist on hiding it, the original need for warmth evolving into desire to see as little of it as possible, allowing us to pretend we are impregnable. Thus the verdict of the writer who, not wanting to admit the fear of the figure with the reaper, says instead that the pictures of semi-clad sexy young ladies are demeaning. If challenged to explain why this is so, though, my guess is that she would have no answer, for really there is none: a fully naked body, in fact, is innocent of ill effect (and sometimes, when shapely, a considerable delight).

But the writer has something still worse to complain of, namely, the ads which help a man become firm in his intention to make love.

Some are nearly "porn," she says. This is difficult for me to understand, my objection to this commercials being quite the opposite. Their subject is sexual intercourse, so one would think they would contain something sexy, but the opposite is true. We see a man and a woman looking at each other in a friendly way. They ride in boats, they take walks, they paint a wall, they do everything but give us an idea that they are feeling desire for each other and soon will, if the man is "ready," get together in the sack. The final outrage, at the end of the ad, shows the two bathing together--but in separate tubs! (Well, they are holding hands, but, I mean . . .)

The lady who wrote the letter would seem not to like anything that smacks of sex: I *assume* she finds both acceptable in private, but to be naked, to be aroused where we can see, well no. I have to confess I, enjoying the attractiveness of the human form (at its best), and not at all afraid of the fact that we are made to copulate, must disagree.

Richard Lettis

2015, June, Additional Entry

From: *The Record,* June:

Argument: See answering letter..

Additional Entry: June:

The reply:

Memorial

The recent Memorial Day brought forth a letter in which the writer suggested that "We should also have remembered those who fought against us." This predictably brought forth another letter angrily denouncing the "evil" idea. The suggestion was not only wrong but dangerous, a "foolish idea" diverting our attention from the brave men of our own armed forces to think of "the people who kill them." The two letters raise an issue of great importance: should we think of ourselves as the good guys and all who warred against us as the bad guys, or should we regard them simply as young men who fought for their countries as ours did for our country, and find it in us to forgive and to think of them as worthy of our compassion?

When stripped of its hyperbole, the second letter is difficult to argue against: many of the countries which fought us were governed by evil minded men who, had they triumphed, would have brought disaster upon us all. The battle in which we are now engaged is a powerful example, its leaders perpetrating atrocities and threatening to force their ideology upon other countries. But are we sure we can blame their soldiers for obeying these leaders and waging a war, however terribly wrong? When this war is over, is it conceivable that our soldiers might forgive those soldiers and even engage in meeting them and discussing the war?

An answer may be found in another war, one as fierce, as disastrous, as those of the present conflict. But some time ago American soldiers initiated contact with Japanese soldiers: they met and talked and discussed their own parts in the battles, and they found that they could respect and associate with each other — nothing evil or dangerous or wrong resulting. They were not concerned with which side was right, which governments were condemnable; they were simply men who had gone through a terrible experience and now realized that it was something they had shared, had had in common. (One may add to this a single soldier, the hero of Laura Hildebrand's "Unbroken," who looked up the guards in his concentration camp and forgave them all.)

For too long we wretched humans have thrived upon hatred of anything that is different from us: the color of skin, the sex, the nationality, the contrary idea, the different religion. It may be said that these compassionate soldiers, and the writer of the first letter, have decided that the "we" are the good guys and "they" are the bad ones kind of thinking has led us into far more danger and destruction than anything the second letter could imagine. We may find in history the gradual replacing of "we" and "they" with "us," struggling to leave behind fear and hatred, to be replaced with compassion and understanding. There is a French saying that is relevant: "tout comprendre c'est tout pardonner" — to know all is to forgive all. I think that one of the greatest men in our history would have liked that; his name was Jesus.

Richard Lettis

Richard Lettis, Ph.D

2015, August 4th, Additional Entry

Additional Entry: August 4:

Article:

How should we respond to Gov. Bush's recent comment on the Constitution? He said that he sees nothing in the document concerning the rights of gay people, and no doubt he is right. But is it the implication of his statement that therefore gays have no rights? If so, several serious questions must be answered: since the rights of the black race are also not mentioned, did we err in freeing them from slavery and granting them the rights of all other citizens? I do not believe that women are afforded any rights in the Constitution; shall we take away their right to vote? The governor's comment raises these and several other vital concerns; one must hope that he will provide us with answers anon.

The real question, of course, is whether we should, like Justice Scalia, settle all questions by reference to the Constitution as it stands, or accept the argument that time has raised problems which the Constitution did not anticipate, and therefore we must act according to the best resolution of difficulties we can realize. Indeed, it seems reasonable that some changes and additions to the Constitution are necessary.

Time inevitably produces change; the rules and convictions of any document must be found insufficient for the needs of later years — even the Bible, arguably the greatest source to which we may turn in time of trouble, now contains commandments which we no longer can accept (approval of slavery, the inferiority of women, the destruction of all those of another faith). How could our founding fathers anticipate the problem of fracking, the moral question of drones, the difficulties of immigration? This was well understood by perhaps the greatest of these men, Thomas Jefferson, participator in the writing of the writer of the Constitution and author of the Declaration of Independence, who said that he expected the document to require considerable changes and additions in the future. It may well be agreed that we no longer have the leaders of his stature, but we must be content to work with what and whom we have, strong enough to modify and develop, realizing that some of these changes may have been wrong and willing to replace them as may be necessary. We see today to have lost much of the courage and energy with which our nation began; it is time to regain these qualities.

Richard Lettis

Richard Lettis, Ph.D

2015, August 26th, The Record

From: *The Record,* August:
The argument: See answering letter.
From my head, August 26:
The reply:
How Should We Read the Bible?

As several recent letters have shown, readers of The Record participate in the increasing concern about how the Bible should be read. There would seem to be three possibilities: we should read literally, or we should read figuratively, or we should not read the Bible at all.

The third of these convictions may be dismissed at once: the Bible is one of the great religious works, helping to guide mankind in its attempts to live well and fully. But the question of which of the other two should be preferred is much more difficult. Perhaps the most powerful arguments against literal reading are that a disturbing number of the principles given are no longer acceptable, and that some readers find a number of contradictions which of course make it impossible to accept every word as literally valid.

It is indeed difficult if not impossible for the contemporary reader to accept and obey a number of the injunctions found. We are ordered by the Bible to kill all those who do not share our religious beliefs, and also to kill our children if they are disobedient. We are required to regard gay men and women as sinful, and are instructed in the proper way to treat our slaves. In the thousands of years since the Bible was written, mankind has learned to repudiate such actions and convictions and so these parts of the Bible make it difficult to accept the entire work as literally the word of God.

Almost equally troublesome are the several contradictions to be found in the Bible. Jesus Christ is the Prince of Peace, yet he says "Think not that I come to bring peace unto the world; I come to bring a sword." I consulted an Anglican Bishop about this contradiction; he said that this and several other apparent contradictions pose problems only if we insist on literal reading of the Bible. To him the sword is not merely a sword, but the power of God brought to earth. This explanation is not easy to accept: surely the power of God could be better represented then by a word which connotes only slaughter. And surely the deity would recognize that many innocent readers of the literal conviction would be confused and disturbed by such a word, and possibly encouraged to war upon nonbelievers.

Faithful Christians have not as yet found a way to deal with this and several other contradictions. Some simply aver that the Holy Bible cannot contain contradictions, which of course leaves the matter unsettled. Others argue that proper response is to "pray and study," which is of no help, for prayer does not solve contradictions, and there is nothing to study which can justify them.

The conclusion which must be reached, then, is that this great religious work, like all human effort, contains imperfections, which must rule out the assertions that everything said is neither the word of God nor is figurative reading is in its entirety acceptable.

Richard Lettis

Richard Lettis, Ph.D

2015, September 12th, Addtional Entry

Additional Entry: September 12:

Comment:

Sin Strikes

Since its inception, baseball has had to deal with deeds and events that have marred its good name. Though it has not always done well, it has tried each time to right a wrong and to maintain its reputation.

How is it doing today?

Let's look at the heart of baseball, pitching. The pitcher throws the ball; if it touches the strike zone, it is a strike; if it doesn't, it isn't.

That, at least, used to be how it went with the primary act of the game, and was thought to be unchangeable. But now each un-hit pitch that misses the strike zone isn't necessarily a ball; sometimes it can be a strike.

This is because of the catcher. If he catches the ball outside of the strike zone, he deftly moves his glove into the zone, making the pitch look like a strike. It becomes one, of course, only if the umpire has been fooled by the catcher's moved glove, but one has to conclude that at least some times he is influenced, or catchers wouldn't bother.

But actually from one point of view it doesn't matter whether the umpire is fooled or not: the concern is that the catcher tries to deceive him--every catcher, I believe, and on every non-strike pitch. It's become part of the game--commentators now point out the moving glove, and speculate on the efficiency of the catcher; the move is just a newly developed skill.

Should we accept this new baseball act? Isn't it cheating, the pitcher getting credit despite his failure, the umpire being deceived, and the batter penalized for taking a pitch he knew was a ball? Isn't the entire game adversely affected, and aren't we being schooled in the value of chicanery, and hasn't the game gone wrong to accept it?

It may be argued that I am sliding back into the Boy Scout morality of the past; it may be said that in today's sports, as in everything else, the idea is to win, and it doesn't matter how. But to me cheating remains an offense, and a game in which it occurs quite openly, even draws approval, subjects the beginning of each play to corruption, is sadly regrettable.

It used to be that baseball strove to be an honorable sport, with wrongs chased down and ended.

Not any more.

Richard Lettis

2016, March, Additonal Entry

Additional Entry: March 2016

Article:

One must respect this writer for her love of our country, though not for her self-righteous and abrasive tone: "spoiled brats," "self-important self-absorbed individuals." (Why is it that people cannot disagree without descending into the sewer — have they been influenced by the Republican debates?)

She holds contempt for those who contemplate leaving the country if a Republican candidate is elected president; under no circumstances would she leave her country. But is she not thinking of a country of the past, and can she think of deeply loving it as it is now? Is she not troubled by a political party that since Nixon has begun to change from the admirable party it once was to what it is now, unable in the last two elections to agree upon a candidate and coming perilously close to complete dissolution? Can she deeply love a country in which young black men are murdered by the very police who are sworn to protect them? Is it her country that has fallen behind many other countries in its education, its health system, its economy, and and too many other categories? Can she be content with a Supreme Court that has withdrawn protection of voting rights, has declared that companies are the same as individuals, and may contribute billions of dollars to political candidates, overwhelming the modest contributions that true individuals can make? Is she not troubled by a Republican Congress which almost on the first day of Obama's election committed itself to preventing his reelection, resulting in eight years in which but a fraction of what could have been done managed to be passed? (And can this in any way be attributable to the color of the president's skin?)

We are not what we once were, and while we must compliment those who stay at home and continue to try for improvement, we have no right to sneer at others who can no longer endure the devastation. What we must love is the country we once were and which we may hope to be again.

2016, March, Additonal Entry

Additional Entry: March 2016

Article:

The Wheaton College of Chicago has fired one of its teachers, Larycia Hawkins, because she has stated that Christians and Muslims worship the same God. The reason given for this is that Miss Hawkins' views are inconsistent with the College's "doctrinaire convictions."

The College seems unaware that by this action it has severely damaged its status as an educational institution. Colleges do not have "doctrinaire convictions." They do not have any convictions, but are open to all convictions and opinions brought to their attention. Colleges are the incubators of our thinking, the best place we have for the presentation, examination, and conclusion of ideas. The educational institution which begins with a conviction has, by that act, deprived itself of the opportunity for disinterested discussion.

Equally important is the College's violation of free speech, one of the most important bulwarks of freedom in our country. Every citizen has the right to voice any opinion which does not violate a law: the more objectionable, offensive, or outrageous it may be, the greater our need to see that the speaker must be given freedom and must not be punished — except perhaps by another voice which negates it with a counter opinion. That's what our country is about.

Richard Lettis was born in Springfield, Mass. He earned a B.A. at the University of Massachusetts and an M.A. and Ph. D. from Yale. He has taught at Ohio University and Long Island University, where he served as chairman of the English Department and Dean of the College of Arts and Science. He has published two books on Dickens, a pamphlet on J. D. Salinger, and several articles. He is now retired and lives in Ramsey N.J. with his wife, Lucy. He is the proud father of five children, eleven grandchildren, and three great-grandchildren, all superior beings.

richardlettis@optonline.net

Index

Abbas, Mahmoud-89
Afghanistan-32, 36, 59
African-Americans-40,58, 97
Albom,Mitch-43-4
Al-Qaida-33
Amah, Justin, Representative-102
American Civil Liberties Union-15
American Psychiatric Association-28
Anti-Semitism-18
Arkansas-15
Arnold, Matthew-30
Aronsohn, Paul-31
Astarita, Father-50
Assembly Health Committee-70
Atheists-6, 89-90
Atlantic Cape Community College-89
Barbeau, Adrienne-10
Beal, Mittty-88
Bernstein, Barbara-15
Bible, the-10, 54, 79, 96,111
Biden, Joe-95
Bill of Rights-84
Blake, William-5
Blue Laws-79
Boccaccio-11
Boswell, James-22-3
Brights-30
Bush Administration-31, 48, 66
Bush, George W.-31, 32, 36,37,45,64,100,106
Bush, Jeb, Governor-108,111
Bucco, Anthoy, State Senator-55
California-15
Carter, Jimmie-38-9
Catholic Church-24-5, 29, 49, 50,104,105
Caulfield, Holden-8, 9
Caulfield, Phoebe-8
Censorship-7, 8, 14
Centeno, Lind a-2
Cervantes-52
Chaffetz, Jason-102
Chicago Tribune-64
Civil rights-56
Cheney, Dick-31, 95
Christian-53
Children-8, 10
Chinese government-33, 64
Christian, Christmas-3, 29, 78-9, 80, 84, 89
Christie, Chris, Governor-91, 93, 99,108
Chuman, Josepph-26
Clinton Administration-31
Clinton, Hillary-47,108-9
Clinton, William-32
Cold Spring Harbor-6
College of New Jersey-88
Communists-6
Conservatism-48, 63
Constitution-75, 85,104
Contraception-25
Cuba-104

Cummings, Elijah E.-101
C. W. Post Collegial Federation-12
Darwin, Charles-15, 50
Dawkins, Richard-90
Death Penalty-54-5, 69-70
Declaration of Independence-111
Democracy, Democrats-6, 7, 38, 64,68,94-5,100
Deo, Len-85-6
Dickens, Charles-18
Don Quixote-52
Drew University-88
Ecconomy-48
Eden-17
Egyptians-42-3
Einstein, Albert-30
Eliot, T.S.-18
Ellison, Ralph-27
Euthemasia-98-9
Evolution-15
Essex Country Colege-88
Fitzgerald, F. Scott-16
Free speech-43-5
Galileo-49
Gessen, Masha-77
God-6, 49, 68, 70,79-80,96
Gospels-54
Greenwald, Louis-93
Ground Zero-53
Gruber, Jonathan,99-101
Guns-71-2, 78,81,91,93
Hamlet-8
Hannukah-80
Hatch, Orrin-26
Hauck, Steven-89
Hawaii-15
Holland-76
Health-care law-62
Homophobia, Homosexuals-40, 53-4, 56, 58, 61, 73-75
House Committee on Oversight and Government Reform-101
Guns-77
Iraq-32, 59, 64
Islam-106
Issa Darrel, Representative-101
Jefferson, Thomas-6,111
Jersey City Police Department-92
Jesus Christ-6, 53. 80 ,86, 96
Jews-58, 97,109-10
Johnson, Samuel-22-3
Julius, Anthony-18
Kass, John-64-5
Kintz, Jarpd-98
Knox,Viki-53
Kwanzaa-80
Lanza, Adam-91
Laurence, D. H-10
Leahy, George-14
Lettic, Lucy-52
Liberals-62
Libya-45
Limbaugh, Rush-57-8
Lockett, Khalil-89

Long Island-6, 8, 19
Long Island Railrooaad-23-4
Mainwaring, Doouglas-74
"Male Survivor"-83
Massachusetts Institute of
Technology-101
"Maude"-10
McCain, John-26
McClatchy-Tribune-43
McGrath, Charles-22
McGuire, Mark-22
Meezan, Wiliam-77
Mercer County Community College-88
Meyer, Toni-61,74-5
Morgan, Arthur-55
Muslim-58,105-6,109-10
NAACP-27
National Debt-64
National PTA-10
National Relations Board-12
Navy-40
New Hampshire-15
New Jersey Death with Dignity Act-70
New Jersey Family Policy Council-85
New Jersey Scholarship and Transformative Education in Prison-88
Netherlands Study on Gay Marriage76
New Mexico-15
Newsday-4, 5, 7, 10, 12
New York Police Department-8
Notre Dame-49
Obama, Barack-26,32,36,37,42,43,45-47,48,62,63,64,68,82,94-5,99,100,103,104,105,106
Old Testament-96
Osama bin Laden-64, 66-7
Osmond, Dony-10
Osmond, Marie-10
Palin, Sarah-226
Parents-10, 11
Paris-105
Paul, Apostle-60, 84
Peres, Shimon-89
Petraeus, David-36
Phelps family (Fred)-43
Pledge of allegiance-56
Pope, Alexander-6, 29
Pope, Francis-86, 89-90,104
Post College-13
Princeton University-88
Prison-59-60
Prometheus-5
Puerto-Riicans-40
Rahner, Karl-13
Raritan Valley Community College-88
Read, Harry-104
Reading-8, 10
Regnerus, Mark-73-5
Religion-70
Religious Freedom-84-5
Religious Freedom Restoration
Act-85
Republican Governor Association-91
Republicans-37, 38, 46 , 62, 64-7, 94-5

Rodriguez, Amarilis-88
Roosevelt, Franklin D.-64
Romney, George-63,103
Rouch, Jonathan-77
Russell, Rober-50-52
Salem Community Colege-88
Same-sex marriage-27, 61, 73-4
Sandy Hook-91, 93
Santiago, Melvin-92
Second Amendment-71, 77, 93
Sex-3,6,7,8,9,10,11,15,24,25,27,29,32,40,41,43,45,52,53,54,56,57,58,59-60,61,82-4,96,110
Sisman, Adam-22
Snyder, Albert-43
Snyder, Matthew-43
Sosa, Sammy-22
Spain-37
Spanish Inquisition-90
Sports Illustrated-106-7
St. Jpseph Parish-50-
Supreme Court-62
Syria-81-2
Taliban-33
Taxes-12
Teaches Unions-13
Tea Party-34 , 63, 94
Ten Commandments-86
Texas-13, 15
"The Tiger"-5
Tokyo-105
Tolerance-53
Vietnam War-12
Salinger, J. D.-8
Sandy Hook-93
Sex-6, 41, 57
Shakespeaare-10
Shelley, Percy -15
Singer, Robert, State Senator-55
"Songs of Experience"-7
"Songs of Innocence"-7
State of the Union Adress-46
Suburban News Port Washington-41
Supreme Court-43-4
"The Lamb"-7
"The Catcher in the Rye"-8
"The God delusion"-90
"The Graduate"-82
"The Great Gatsby"-16
"The Invisible Man-27
The New Yorker-18
The New York Times-4, 14, 15, 17, 19, 21, 22, 23, 24, 30
The New York Times Book Review-22
The New York Times Magazine-13
The
Record-28,29,30,31,32,35,36,37,38,39,40,43,44,45,47,48,49,52,53,54,56,57,58,59,60,62,64,65,67,68,71,72,74,78
,79,80,81,83,84,85,86,90,91,93,95,96,98,100,103,106,109,11187,
The Tea Party-46
The Tiger"-5
The Vatican-103
Trump, Donald-47
The United States-6
University of Texas-73-5Vatican-89

Voltare-13
Waiters-19-20
Wallace, Alfred Russell-50
"War and Peace-19
Westboro Baptist Church, 43-4, 85
Women-58
Yale Alumni Magazine-27, 97
Yale University-97
Yeats, W. B.-30
Xiridou, Maria-76

Acknowledgments

I am grateful to Ms. Donna Blair, of the Digital Archives Department, North Jersey Media Group, for her patience and for the many letters she located and sent to me. But of course my greatest thanks must be for my wife, Lucy Young Bara Lettis, who provided so many kinds of help, from finding letters to giving practical and emotional support for an effort that turned out to be rather longer and more difficult than I had anticipated.